MEDIA STRATEGIES

FOR INTERNET MARKETERS

How to Use Publicity + Offline Exposure to Drive
More Traffic & Increase Conversions Online

PETE WILLIAMS

MEDIA STRATEGIES FOR INTERNET MARKETERS:
How to Use Publicity + Offline Exposure
to Drive More Traffic & Increase Conversions Online

Published by Preneur Marketing
Suite 2, 284 St Kilda Rd, St Kilda 3182 Victoria, Australia
www.PreneurMarketing.com

Printed in the United States of America

ISBN-13: 978-0615499789
ISBN-10: 0615499783

Visit the Media Strategies for Internet Marketers website at:
www.MediaStrategiesForInternetMarketers.com

To my Virtual Team,
You know who you are... I wouldn't be me without you.

PART ONE
Why you should be generating offline publicity for your online business in real world media

What is this book all about?

Are you running an online business? Are you looking for an easy way to increase your sales and make more money? If so, you'll be pleased to discover that this book is for you!

If you have a web-based business, you should really consider generating offline publicity in newspapers, magazines and trade journals to increase web traffic and your conversion rates.

Publicity (also referred to as PR – Public Relations) in real world media adds value to your business increasing your bottom line, generating new viewers to your website and opening more opportunities to target new prospects.

PLUS, publicity also gives you additional benefits explained later in this book that will increase your online conversion rates – GUARANTEED!

Media Strategies for Internet Marketers will clearly show you how effective PR can:

- direct more customers to your website and increase your level of traffic
- improve your leads and attract a bigger audience
- dramatically increase your sales conversion rate
- make this all happen with minimal time and effort, and without spending a cent!

Although this book is primarily written for business-owners running an online business (i.e. those who make a living and earn income through the internet), the lessons you'll learn can be taken away and used by any business owner or entrepreneur in the real world. *Media Strategies for Internet Marketers* can help improve any business and increase sales, regardless what type of business you're running.

Free publicity: the secret to successfully running an online business and giving up your day job

Like most online marketers, you probably started your blog, e-commerce store or niche website in an effort to make more money and replace your day job. But if you're like the 99% of 'online marketers' out there, unfortunately this hasn't happened yet.

Why is this? Well, firstly let me tell you it's NOT YOUR FAULT.

None of the 'gurus' out there have taught you to think of your website or blog as a business. As unfortunate as that might sound, that's the truth. You'll find that every internet marketer out there that has successfully managed to replace their day job has learnt to treat their website like a real business – not just a hobby with the long-term goal of replacing income.

See, most entrepreneurs usually start out running online businesses selling services, products or books as something to do in their spare time. In the end, the business doesn't grow because the owner doesn't treat their business like a real world business.

If you really want to embrace the opportunity to make more money from your e-commerce site, get serious about running a real world business. Market your business properly and successfully – don't just treat your business like a something on the side of your normal daily working life. If you never treat it like a real business, your business won't expand.

But don't let this concept of 'getting serious' scare you – it's easy to make your online business a real world business. The best way to get started is to go offline, and *Media Strategies for Internet Marketers* is designed to show you how you can make this happen.

This book is not about making you work any harder to achieve your goals; this book is about teaching you how to work smarter. Publicity will help your online sales soar, and this book will cover EXACTLY how to do this step-by-step, without putting in any extra effort.

Relying on your website as your only marketing strategy

There are countless online businesses that do not think of publicity when coming up with a marketing strategy to increase sales. Why?

Because when business owners and online marketers start online businesses, they focus on only one aspect of the marketing mix: their website.

Focusing only on the internet instantly sets you up for failure. Treating the internet as your only one path to market limits the number of people that your business can potentially connect with, and you don't reach nearly as many people who might be interested in what you have to sell.

As a business owner, you put yourself at a huge disadvantage if you rely on the internet as your only marketing strategy. Directing all of your marketing efforts to reach an online audience is only one way to promote your business.

Although solely marketing your business via the internet is possible, you waste of a lot of potential opportunities and unnecessarily limit the number of people that you will reach. To really succeed in increasing traffic and sales conversions, you need to get as many leads as possible through promoting your business in different ways.

Reach beyond the online world for leads

Business owners tend to put their blinkers on and forget to reach beyond the internet for different leads, If you want to increase traffic to your site, don't solely rely on online strategies. Various lead sources are crucial for businesses to survive.

You might be thinking: *"But my website does create a lot of different leads! Banner advertising, SEO, affiliate marketing..."* OK, sure, but let's take a closer look.

Banner advertising, SEO and affiliate marketing might all be different lead sources, but they all do the same thing – target online internet users. We tend to forget that people are still influenced by watching television, listening to the radio, and reading newspapers and magazines.

If you can reach out to potential customers offline, you can easily generate more leads to your business simply by targeting a wider audience. Remember that there is a real business behind your computer that needs promoting, so you should treat it like any other 'bricks and mortar'-type business and start taking advantage of the fact that there are more people offline than online.

Tip: Check out this real world example!

Here is a copy of an article in the newspaper titled "Online training program helps to fight puppy fat". It was featured in The Weekend Post, and covers how dogs are now becoming overweight.

Take a closer look at the article and you'll notice that online business <www.poochto5k.com> has used this article as a way to not only inform readers of this canine obesity problem, but to also promote their new dog training program.

The article clearly encourages readers to visit their website, which will increase traffic to their site, and eventually increase their sales!

So how did they get this publicity in the newspaper? They sent a press release to The Weekend Post of course!

Read on to find out how you can do this for yourself.

Internet users VS people who use the internet

It could be argued that nowadays, everyone uses the internet, so why bother searching for leads offline?

The answer lies here in the simple but crucial fact that there are two types of people who use the internet:

1. Regular internet users – people who are often online and use the internet for most of their needs, such as online banking and searching directories.
2. People who use the internet – people who live mostly in the offline world but occasionally use the internet to check their email or Facebook account.

These users are NOT THE SAME, and there is a huge difference between the way they use the internet. As a business, you must realise that everyone may have used the internet before, but not everyone uses the internet.

To help explain, just because someone has an email address does not make them an internet user. Someone who has created a Facebook profile or a Gmail account simply *uses* the internet from time to time. The difference is that unlike regular internet users, they don't spend time searching for information, products of services they want online.

It's key to understand that not everyone is **on** the internet **all** the time. People who just sometimes use the internet to check their email or Facebook:

- don't Google search what they want online
- don't browse websites
- don't read blogs
- or go shopping when they're online.

So, because these people still search for things offline, you can see there are tons of prospects you can target beyond the internet. Remember, you're running a real life business that you depend on to generate income. Don't limit your website to only an online audience. Get out there and start promoting your business to the rest of the world!

Tip: Direct Mail

Marketing plans that successfully reach out to offline audiences often include Direct Mail.

What is Direct Mail? Direct Mail is marketing material personally addressed to a recipient – a subscriber, member or particular prospect. It can include newsletters, brochures, postcards or flyers.

Many businesses tend to forget that Direct Mail has successfully been running for the past 50-60 years. Why? Because it works – it's all about sending an effective message to a large targeted offline audience. It is this principle that all foolproof sales and marketing strategies are based on.

So what is publicity?

Publicity is when your business is exposed to the public via a range of media. 'The public' can mean anything from your local community to an international audience, and coverage in the media can include:

- a short story televised on the news
- an interview broadcast over the radio
- a report published in the newspaper, or
- an article that you wrote for a magazine.

In thinking about the content required to generate this publicity, there are two different ways you can go about it. You can either:

1. be the content (when the publicity is about your service or product) or
2. provide the content (when the publicity is provided by you).

We will investigate these two concepts in much more detail in Parts Two and Three of this book!

How does publicity help my business?

Generating publicity helps to expand your business by increasing traffic, sales and conversions. *'How?'* I hear you ask. Let me explain.

Here are the ways in which publicity will help convert your viewers into sales:

- It will increase your exposure in the real world (not just the internet!) and raise brand awareness amongst potential customers.
- It will help your business build a credible reputation, leading more customers to trust in your brand and purchase from you compared to your competitors.
- It will consequently fuel more and more sales for your business, increasing your market share and income.

What makes publicity so magical is that the media chooses to turn your business into an interesting story; you do not pay for this type of publicity, the media chooses to promote you. It is important to understand that your feature story is not a *paid advertisement*. Audiences are more likely to connect with your business as you are presented as a real story, not just another ad. Better yet, the best thing about publicity is that it is virtually free.

To develop a clearer understanding of why publicity is more effective than advertising, continue reading this book. Part Two and Part Three investigates this topic further, and will teach you how you can use publicity to your advantage.

Why are the opportunities offline so great?

There is a much bigger audience to market to offline than online. As online business managers, we spend most of our time connected to the World Wide Web, and have become so accustomed to sitting in a chair front of a computer that we've forgotten that the outside world still exists.

We just established that there are people who don't regularly use the internet to search for things and make purchases online. But these people are still buyers, they just prefer to search for things that they like offline. They still like to spend money on things that interest them in the real world; these buyers have real world lives and real world interests in niche areas, and continue to live out their personal interests offline.

To help explain, let me give you an example. People who are passionate about guitars don't just use the internet to research and fulfil their hobby. If somebody really loves guitars, they absolutely love guitars. They will live, eat and breathe anything to do with guitars, and will look in places other than just the internet for interesting information. In addition to using the internet (if at all), these buyers will read guitar magazines, watch music-related TV shows, and absorb everything guitar-related in other forms of media as well. And this is where publicity comes into play.

If you sell anything to do with guitars, get your products featured in real world media. You could write an article about it and get it published in a music-related magazine. A die-hard guitar fan is bound to spot your article and will not hesitate to spend their hard-earned money on something that they are passionate about. They will visit your website or Google your business name (because it will be listed in the article), and voila, you have converted your first offline reader into a tangible sale. Remember: a fan is a fan for life, they keep an eye out for whatever they love everywhere they look.

FACT: Offline users are much easier to impress than online users!

Another reason why directing offline customers to your website is so fantastic is because it is so much easier to impress people who aren't regular internet users. Offline customers aren't as jaded or sceptical of the internet as savvy modern-day internet users, so it's easier to convert their visits into sales once you have their full attention.

You see, regular online users are surrounded by the internet all day. They are accustomed to seeing fancy websites all the time, and aren't as easily excited or motivated to make purchases online.

On the other hand, people who aren't regular internet users are often amazed with good looking websites. They're easily impressed, and if they like the way that your business is presented online, they're much more likely to buy from you.

These prospects usually haven't seen auto-responders, squeeze pages or online sales videos before, so when they are first exposed to these ideas, they are much more responsive than the typical online user. Do you remember the first time you received a personalised auto-responder sequence? _Did you hit 'reply' thinking that the email was only sent to you?_

For this reason, your chances of successfully converting these prospects are much higher; you can engage with them more easily and give them the Wow factor that regular users don't care for. Capture their interest and excite them with your special online offers. All you need to do is focus on getting the buyers to your site in the first place.

Gaining credibility in the marketplace

We all know the value of testimonials – they show other people you are capable of providing people with a fantastic service or producing a fantastic product. The use of testimonials to endorse your business is the most common way to gain credibility amongst potential customers, without employing paid advertising or publicity.

But today, testimonials aren't as effective as they used to be. People are sceptical and don't believe in testimonials anymore because they are often seen as fake. After all, anyone can endorse a business – they don't even have to have a real name – so who is to say that these testimonials are real?

To combat this ongoing problem, businesses have recognised that testimonials are more believable if the words come from an industry expert. By choosing a professional to promote your business, consumers are more likely to take the endorsement seriously, as people understand that the expert's reputation is on the line to support the product or service.

However, the ultimate testimonial with the highest success rate is a media endorsement – where you are promoted by TV and radio show hosts, magazine editors and newspaper journalists in the real world.

Media endorsement: the best testimonial you can possibly get

So why is it that people's consumer behaviour can be influenced so much by using publicity? Strangely enough, people trust the media. Consumers are aware that businesses can't really fake or buy that kind of public endorsement. As soon as you are featured in real world media (non-website-based media), the media instantly awards you expert status and you are given a stamp of approval. This is because TV stations don't waste time with boring everyday people; they only talk to interesting, credible experts.

Furthermore, when trying to convert browsers into buyers, publicity works even better than celebrity endorsements, because we all know that celebrity endorsements are paid. Famous people don't vouch for products just because they like them, and they certainly don't have to believe in what they say if they're getting paid to say it! Essentially, publicity works so well because it is not advertising. It is honest.

Publicity VS Advertising

Publicity and advertising are both forms of marketing that aim to achieve the same result – increase brand awareness and generate more sales. However, although they have the same idea, they are both very different. Let's consider these key differences:

Advertising	Publicity
You pay big money to gain the exposure you want	The media chooses to give you the exposure, so it's virtually free!
People are aware that it is a paid advertisement, so your business' marketing message isn't as credible	Because the media chooses to endorse you and your business, you build trust and credibility

Unlike paid advertising, publicity is effective because it is a buzz that is created by the media *about* you. It is not a buzz that is created *by* you.

For this reason, it makes sense that you will succeed in converting more customers into sales using publicity, because people usually don't care for advertisements. From our own personal experience, we know that audiences pay more attention to publicity in the media than advertisements – as consumers, we know that the ads are paid for. We all tend to tune out when we are fed paid marketing messages, but publicity (that buzz *about* you) attracts genuine interest amongst offline audiences, and ultimately helps your business generate more leads.

How do we tap into this offline market?

To take advantage of these offline users, your business needs to expand its marketing strategy and reach out to people using 'real world' media: TV, radio, print and others. This is what we call 'going analogue' – moving away from digital technology back to more traditional forms of media to generate publicity offline.

Throughout this book, you'll learn how to make this happen easily and effectively, in less than 30 minutes per week!

Creating content for publicity

To generate publicity through these offline media outlets, you need to provide them with content. By being featured by the media, you reach various audiences beyond the internet and ultimately promote your business in a more effective way.

Focus on getting in touch with the media by giving them interesting press releases and useful articles. By generating publicity in areas other than the internet, your business builds a presence and credibility across different media forms. This can be done in two ways:

- You can *be* the content, or
- you can provide the content.

The content needs to relate to your business somehow. Make sure you catch the media's attention with something interesting to say, providing new information to different prospects – *don't worry, we cover how to do this later.*

Tell the media about yourself and let them promote you!

Your objective with these press releases and articles is self-promotion. For example, you could tell radio stations that you're a good candidate to be interviewed because you know a lot about an upcoming event. Or you could write an informative article on the latest developments in your field.

Publicity ultimately helps with successful conversion rates because when you are featured in a story, the media gives an endorsement to your business; they take the risk, the due diligence, on behalf of your potential customers to check that you are a reputable source of important information.

Tip: Exposure – the REAL reason why you should be creating content!

Many online businesses already write online articles and blogs to create relevant content and backlinks for their site. This helps your SEO rankings and is a great way for your business to cross-reference other useful online resources and tools.

However, creating content for your website serves a bigger purpose than just improving SEO and backlinks. The real reason why your business should be creating blogs is to gain exposure, generate publicity and earn credibility in the offline world! If you want to get the most out of your writing efforts, get your blog posts published in print and boost your public profile as an expert. You'll reap the rewards in increased conversions immediately!

This type of exposure builds trust. If you can write on the top of your website *"As seen in…"* your reputation becomes validated and approved. Without investing your business' entire budget into a conventional advertising campaign, you're able to use this publicity to help maximise lead generation and profits. You become an authoritative figure in your industry, and if people believe that you are an expert at what you do, they are more likely to buy from you than anyone else.

Publicity is easy – just leverage what content you've already got!

Generating publicity is easy! If you're a savvy online marketer, you probably already have a bunch of online articles and blog posts waiting to be used. Or perhaps you have old newsletters with useful information, or you have some write-ups that you have previously compiled for marketing brochures.

This is exactly the same type of content you can send out to the media! If you can use this, you don't need to do any extra work at all – it's all about leveraging what you've already got. You may need to update or modify your content to tailor each article for different audiences, but for not much extra effort, you reach a much broader range of prospects by repurposing your content for different media forms.

Get more mileage out of what you're already doing to increase traffic and online conversions, without working any harder. It's all about syndicating what you already do in other ways.

"But what if I don't have any content?"

The best thing about creating content is that there is practically no cost other than the investment of time to write the press release or article. If your business does not have an inventory of content ready to go, *Media Strategies for Internet Marketers* will teach you how to create press releases and articles yourself.

Alternatively, if you are too busy to compile the content yourself, I would recommend you outsource any work that you need to do. You could either:

1. hire a virtual assistant (or a real live person) to help you run your business, which will free up your time allowing you to focus on crafting good content, or
2. hire a writer to create the quality content for you, so you don't have to worry about a thing.

Although these two options will require you to outlay some money for labour, the cost of outsourcing this help is an extremely small cost compared to the financial benefits you will reap from effective publicity.

What I am not saying...

So now you can see why generating publicity can be so good for your business. But don't get the wrong idea:

- I am not asking you forget everything that you already know and focus all of your efforts into real world media.
- I am not asking you to stop working on your online marketing – no matter what, any marketing is still marketing and it will help raise the profile of your business in some way.
- I am not saying that online marketing won't get you anywhere – Google AdWords is still an effective way of attracting prospects to your website.
- I still think that while you try to generate offline publicity, you should continue to take

Tip: Increase your prices!

You might be thinking that you have no desire to generate publicity because you are already busy enough as it is. After all, your sales are going considerably well.

Well, let me ask you: are you interested in making more money? If so, generating publicity does more than just generate immediate sales; it also generates long-lasting credibility and trust.

This means that you can afford to increase your selling price without losing business, because if your business has a good reputation, people will still be willing to buy from you. Make more money without investing any more time, effort or resources into your business. How easy is that?!

advantage of online leads sources to further grow your business online.

What I am definitely saying, however, is that generating publicity via TV, radio and print is just one sure-fire way of reaching more prospects, increasing your traffic and improving your conversion rate, ultimately helping you and your business make more money.

Why take my advice? Let me tell you about my experience...

So you're probably asking yourself, *"Why should I listen to this guy? Will what he says really work?"*

Let me introduce myself. My name is Pete Williams, and ever since I was young, I've always had an entrepreneurial streak. As a teenager I used to set up stalls and I even wrote my own newsletters to people in my local community. Now, in my twenties, I have:

- been dubbed as "Australia's Richard Branson"
- authored international smash hit *How To Turn Your Million Dollar Idea Into A Reality*
- been Global Runner Up in the JCI Creative Young Entrepreneur Awards 2009
- been Southern Regional Finalist in the Ernst & Young Entrepreneur Awards 2010
- become a member of Smart Companies: Top 30 Under 30

I currently own several different real world businesses and websites, including Infiniti Telecommunications, On Hold Advertising, Simply Headsets and the Preneur Group. (For a full list and bio, you can check out my website: www.preneurmarketing.com)

I have always worked hard to promote these companies and websites using publicity as a major tool to drive people through my doors. Calling upon this experience, I have decided to write this book in the hope that I can encourage other businesses to do the same.

Generating publicity offline in real world media has worked for me time and time again, and I have experienced the benefits of this type of PR firsthand. My goal is to help you improve your leads offline, just as I have done with my businesses, ultimately helping you drive additional business to your website.

The MCG: Back to where my publicity experience began

When I was 21 years old, I read the book *One Minute Millionaire* by Robert Allen and Mark Victor Hansen. In this book is the story of Paul Hartunian, who had the brilliant idea of salvaging timber from the famous Brooklyn Bridge while it was being redeveloped in the

1980s. Hartunian then cut up the timber he had managed to collect from the walkway of the bridge and sold them as souvenirs for US$14.95 each, with 5" x 11" certificates that he'd made himself, outlining the history of the bridge. This simple and unique venture ended up making him over US$2 million.

After reading this story, I wondered how I could replicate this venture in Australia. At the time, Australia's number one sporting ground, the MCG, was undergoing redevelopment. I quickly took action and tracked down the wrecking company involved, and discovered that not only did they have a significant amount of timber, but they also had a considerable amount of the world-famous MCG Crested Carpet, which originally lay in the members' dining room.

After viewing the carpet lying in the corner of the wreckers' warehouse the following morning, I took the entire sum along with a mass of timber at a very 'pleasing' price, and developed a series of limited edition sports memorabilia pieces which sold from $395 to $1495. These included a photo of the MCG, a piece of the famous carpet and even a limited number series that had their frame created out of the timber, which was once the stadium.

How do I tell people my story with no marketing budget?

At the time, I had no marketing budget. I was only 21 years old, with zero capital to spend. I couldn't afford to advertise, so I decided to contact as many people as I could to tell my story.

I distributed a press release (that cost me zero dollars) with the headline '21 Year Old Sells MCG For Under $500'. Almost immediately, it attracted huge amounts of publicity and generated over $50,000 of free advertising and publicity in the media via Channel 7 News, articles in the Herald Sun, AM and FM Radio interviews and trade magazine articles.

The best thing was that the more exposure I received, the more sales I made. I was even dubbed by the media as "Australia's Richard Branson", which lifted my public profile as an entrepreneur and benefited my business ventures immeasurably. The publicity generated a huge proportion of my profit at absolutely no cost. I did not pay big bucks for this kind of attention — all it cost me was a little time.

This is why getting publicity is so great — it is not only incredibly helpful in generating interest and ultimately sales, but it is also much more cost-effective than conventional advertising, and can offer even better results.

What you'll get out of this book

There are two essential keys required for any business to work:

Tip: The more the merrier!

1. traffic to your website, and
2. conversions.

Send your press release out to as many people as you can – you never know what kind of results you could achieve. I sent my press release to a friend who then passed it on to someone else and I was eventually called up for an interview on Today Tonight, which was broadcast to a nationwide audience. This created a huge boom for my business and straight away sales went through the roof!

To make this happen, you need to generate publicity. If you can become visible in the offline world, you can lure potential customers who do not regularly use the internet to visit your website and get them to buy from you once they are there. Getting this attention is what *Media Strategies for Internet Marketers* is all about.

Media Strategies for Internet Marketers will help you figure out everything you need to know involved with getting publicity, starting with questions such as:

- Who is my target market?
- Where do these people get their information?
- How do I write a press release or an article?
- How do I know who to pitch it to?
- What's the best way to send it out to people?

You'll also learn how to put systems in place to help you leverage your time as much as possible. You'll learn that it doesn't take much to increase the mileage of what you already do, and generate infinite benefits for your business and your income.

If you can generate publicity in offline media, I guarantee that you will improve the amount of traffic to your website and increase your online conversion rate.

This book will teach you how to get started and make it all happen today.

PART TWO
Being the Content

What does it mean to BE the content?

'Being' the content means that you are the content (or the subject) of the publicity. You are the person who gets talked to, or talked about, that is interviewed or featured in the media.

If you can secure an interview with the media, it is your golden opportunity to go all-out promoting yourself and your business. It's your chance to discuss your story, your achievements, and share your ideas with different audiences to generate interest in what you do.

How does publicity actually increase my conversion rate?

I hear you asking, *"But how does going offline with an interview like this actually increase my sales conversions?"* Well, it's as simple as recognising that consumers are more inclined to buy if they can see that the business has already been endorsed by someone else.

When looking at a website, customers ask themselves:

- How can I trust this person?
- How do I know they are a real business that will deliver exactly what I want?
- Can they support me, give me customer service when I need it, and answer all my queries if need be?

Essentially, these customers want to know that your business is trustworthy and dependable before they consider spending their hard-earned cash with you. Publicity is a form of marketing that increases your conversion rate by establishing this trusting relationship for you.

Establish your reputation and become a market leader

Generating publicity in the media is more than just getting an article published in a magazine. Generating publicity helps you become a market leader in your industry.

As soon as potential customers stumble across your website, they'll be able to see that you have been featured by the media. By making it clear on your site that you've been endorsed by the media, you can gain credibility and establish a reputation as a professional. Consumers become confident that if you're good enough to be interviewed, you're able to deliver exactly what customers want.

Because of this endorsement, customers are immediately more likely to purchase from you compared to someone they've never heard of before, whether they actually read your interview or not. They can see the legitimate connection without seeing your article printed – the media has done the due diligence in endorsing you as a reliable expert in your field.

Keep in mind that when you're featured in the media, it is the media who endorses you. Your interview is not an advertisement. As mentioned in Part One, although editorial and advertising both aim to generate interest, they are completely different. An interview in the media helps you build a solid reputation; the media portrays you as a reliable and trustworthy business. Most importantly the endorsement is not paid, so it is credible and honest. That's priceless approval in the marketplace that advertising just can't buy.

What you'll learn in this section

To find out more about 'being' the content, this section will teach you how to promote yourself, show you how to write and distribute your own press releases, and go into further detail how this will benefit your business. Topics covered include:

- What the Halo Effect is, and how does it help you?
- How do I get that publicity happening in the first place?
- What is a press release for?
- How do I write an interesting press release that people will want to read?
- How do I distribute my press release, and get the best response rate possible?

The Halo Effect

If you are the content, you are the subject or the topic of the publicity. You are the person who is interviewed for your story, experience, expertise and knowledge of whatever field of business you're in. Because this media feature is not an advertisement, the publicity created about you produces "The Halo Effect".

The Halo Effect is exactly what it sounds like. If you're featured in real world media, you're awarded an angel's halo because you're an expert (not an advertiser!). Your interview in the media provides an objective opinion, a third party testimonial or third party endorsement, and by being positively represented in the media, your audience will look up to you and believe what you have to say is honest, credible and trustworthy.

The Halo Effect is very powerful at influencing people's buying decisions and works astonishingly well because you are able to capture the audience's attention with engaging human-interest stories, in which you present viewers with expert advice, hints, inside tips and useful solutions. For this reason, the audience believes that you are telling your story because it is genuinely interesting, not because you are trying to sell something.

If we take a step back and look at why the concept of testimonials works so well, we can see that consumers are comforted to know that there are other people like them who have the same interests who have dealt with the same business and have survived, with little or no complaints. This concept is called 'social proof', a term coined from the famous book *Influence: The Psychology of Persuasion*, written by the acclaimed American psychologist, Robert Cialdini.

Social proof

Social proof ties in with The Halo Effect because by being featured in offline media, the media saves your audience 'due diligence'. Due diligence is the act of having to research and experience something for yourself; or in other words, going through with the risk of buying something from a business they know nothing about. The Halo Effect reassures customers that although they have absolutely no prior knowledge or experience of your business, you are someone that they can trust.

Once you are able to secure this kind of publicity in the media, you're then able to take advantage of the opportunity to promote your business by clearly adding: "As featured in…" or "Regular columnist for…" to your website. This form of 'social proof' allows customers to tell themselves: "If someone else can do it that's not me, then this business must be alright." Remember that by being endorsed by the media, you are clearly portrayed as a market leader in your field. You have been chosen by the media to be interviewed instead of everyone else in the same business as you.

Such third party endorsements legitimise your expertise as a reputable and reliable real world business, resulting in much higher conversions once you're able to draw people to your site. What's more, this social proof can help you to make more money without lifting a finger by enabling you to sell the same products/services at a higher selling price.

Making the publicity happen

So now you understand why publicity is so good for business. People are attracted to you because you're not an advertiser; you have something interesting and useful to say, and you build trust in the public eye by being endorsed by the media. Now it's time to look at how to make this happen in the first place. How do you get someone interested in interviewing you?

First and foremost, you need to write a press release. It is important for you to be aware that big commercial media outlets connect with millions of people, so they get contacted with stories all the time. This means that the chances of your press release getting picked up by big media companies are pretty slim because they can afford to be more selective about who they choose to interview. So, it's a good idea to start with local media as your first target and build from there.

Starting out small

When most people think of publicity in the media, they automatically think of big interviews staged in front of live audiences such as *Oprah* or the *Late Show with David Letterman*. But the reality is that unless you're already a celebrity, you're probably not going to get interviewed on prime time TV. Think of it this way: the bigger the audience, the harder it is for you to get an interview.

Let's face it – the chances of scoring publicity on national TV or radio are pretty slim. However, getting publicity in the media is not impossible! Don't forget that there are magazines, newspapers and trade journals out there that are just as popular and always on the lookout for quality content.

These media outlets have smaller (but just as dedicated) niche audiences and are more likely to publish a story about you. It's important to remember that when you're starting out, you need to take baby steps – start small, and work your way to the top. Magazines, newspapers and trade journals are the most common forms of publicity, and contacting these groups first is the easiest way to start generating publicity and build your reputation as a professional in your field.

And, in addition to giving you the best opportunity to build a great folio, starting out small allows you to get the best PR practice. It's the perfect way to prepare for future interviews – it helps to build your confidence and publicity skills, and you'll be able to call upon this interview experience and nail the interviews with bigger audiences when they come around.

Making the most of what you've got

Once you're publicised in a small newspaper or regional radio, you can ride on the back of this publicity and slowly grow, leveraging off whatever small amount of exposure you can get. You will see a continued flow-on effect if you use these press clippings in your folio to your advantage. The fact that you have already been publicised somewhere will show other media outlets that you're getting attention with something interesting to say, and this helps you score even more publicity reaching out to even more people.

In time, you will slowly become more visible in the public sphere. You can start to give yourself a byline, making you sound more important, such as "As featured in…" Sound familiar? This is the 'social proof'/Halo Effect that we talked about earlier, where once you're able to tell prospects you've been featured in the media, you're awarded a halo for your good work. All these things build trust with the consumer and encourage them to buy from you.

Before you get started...

- Before you begin writing your press release, there are several important things you should know.
- The aim of the press release is to get you an interview only – not tell your life story. You will get the opportunity to talk further in length once you score the interview.
- Before you write your press release, remember you're trying to pitch quality content. Make it clear that you are worth interviewing because you have something new and interesting to say, and you have something useful and important to contribute to their audience.
- KISS: Keep It Short and Simple. Maximise your chances of being picked up by making sure your press release is only one page long and double-spaced. It is a big myth that you have to tell the media your life story to get them interested in you. The truth is that you don't have to write much at all. Journalists are very busy people, and if your press release contains too many words, they'll instantly think it's too long and won't bother reading it.
- A press release is just a sales letter selling YOU. Your objective is to sell yourself as the interviewee, an expert in whatever industry you're in. The same salesmanship principles apply here as with any other sales material.

Getting attention and creating headlines

If you want to be picked up by the media, you need to prove to them that you have something exciting to say. Journalists are often bombarded with stories, and it's up to them to decide which ones are more newsworthy than others. To make sure your press release doesn't get thrown in the bin straight away, capture their attention with a flashy, eye-catching headline. Like every good sales letter, you need a headline that grabs the journalist's attention. Then be sure to back this up with equally engaging content to maintain their interest.

To create the most effective press release, start by asking yourself, "So, what subject am I going to talk about?" This should be easy – it's your area of expertise! It's important that you pick a niche topic you are able to talk about with expert knowledge and authority. Remember, the aim of the press release is to increase your public profile by being portrayed as a specialist in your field.

Researching what your audiences want

Once you're able to identify what you're good at talking about, you'll then need to ask yourself, "What do I write about?"

Deciding the content and topic of your press release and figuring out what purpose it serves to your readers scares everyone, but it's a lot easier than you think. It's just a matter of becoming as focused as possible on quality content by brainstorming ideas, and most importantly, researching what people are interested in.

The core idea behind researching what your audience wants is: it's not about *figuring* out your content, it's about *finding* your content. You shouldn't have to think of a topic on your own. If you want to know all the topics that people want to read about, all you have to do is look. Get to know your target market, and provide them with content that they will want to read. Figure out what type of advice they seek, or what common questions they usually have.

Here are some important pointers to help you figure it out.

Using your email list

As an entrepreneur, you should already have an email list of prospects. These prospects might be former customers, or leads that haven't purchased from you but have subscribed to your regular newsletters.

Get the most out of your email lists by contacting them for help. Asking them questions by surveying your current database is the easiest way to get good content – you don't have to come up with the idea, just find it.

Take advantage of this resource, and email them with intriguing questions, such as "What's your biggest concern with…?" or "What do you like most about…" If you do not have a list, start creating one today!

Surveys & questionnaires

The easiest way is to start with your existing database. Finding answers are easy and guaranteed to find something to write about from the responses you'll receive. In order to get a hold of this information, start with surveys to conduct research. A fantastic online tool that anyone can use is Survey Monkey, a service that helps create and distribute surveys for you (better yet, if you only have 10 questions or less, the service is absolutely free!).

Forum crawling

Another way to conduct research is by checking out what people are saying online. Read up on as many relevant community forums and blogs as you can, and see what comments are being posted up online. This will give you a good indication of how consumers feel about similar products/services in the marketplace, and what kind of feedback they are throwing out there.

All you have to do is Google-search these niche sites to find out what's going on.

Yahoo Answers

You can also find out what types of questions are circulating online by checking in with Yahoo Answers. This website is specifically designed as an online question/answer forum and clearly displays the latest questions that people are asking each other in cyberspace about real life topics. Yahoo Answers goes that one step further and categories these questions for you, so you don't waste time browsing discussions that aren't relevant to your niche. (While visiting the site, you may even want to answer some questions on the spot, which could potentially provide you with some additional leads!)

Google Alerts

One of the easiest ways to stay in touch with what's going on in your niche is signing up for Google Alerts. Google Alerts tells you what is hot in your field of expertise by monitoring specific search terms that you have entered upon sign up. Once you register (it's free), Google Alerts will send you email notifications on your chosen topic directly to your inbox, including coverage across all media forms such as blogs and video. This option is great for those who don't have much time, as you don't need to worry so much about collecting independent research. With Google Alerts, the news comes to you.

Independent observation

You can also conduct valuable research by being observant and sensitive to what everyday people are saying around you in everyday situations. Simple as that. All you have to do is remember that the objective of investing time and effort into research is to find out what people want to know and are interested in. Use the findings from your research to create a press release with content that is relevant to your niche; find out what their problems and concerns are so you can sell answers back to them in the form of a catchy story, full of helpful solutions.

Creating your hook

Once you discover what people might be interested in, use these ideas to create your hook. A hook is an angle that you use to pitch your press release and provoke the reader's attention. A hook is similar to a headline, but more so, it is the original idea behind the content. You can incorporate this hook in the headline of your press release to highlight the message that you are trying to convey.

On top of the research you have conducted within your niche, you should ask yourself questions such as "Have I created or discovered any exciting new products lately that people will want to know about?" or "Have I got a secret or a brand new idea that can help lots of people?"

These kinds of questions will help you clearly define your hook. For example, are you a successful business owner wanting to share your professional experience with other like-minded entrepreneurs? Are you a personal trainer, wanting to share information about a new and exciting way to get fit? Maybe you're a real estate agent wanting to divulge up-to-the-minute advice on what the most rapidly developing and valuable suburbs are in town.

In addition, ask yourself, "What expert opinions can I provide that are relevant to current affairs?" People love to watch / listen / read about topical content. Integrate your professional knowledge with what's going on in the world. By keeping up with the news, you can sell your personal expertise to the media by offering opinion and insight.

When you have finally figured out your headline and what you're going to write, you will then need to send your press release out to relevant niche media outlets. However, have a think about your content. You might find that your expertise is useful across many different niches.

Try to maximise the return of your press release by tweaking your hook, or the angle of your press release to suit different audiences. Changing your hook to suit different media outlets is simply giving different audiences across various niches what they want to hear in different ways. This way, you can send it out to as many people as possible, meaning you have the potential to generate more publicity across a wider audience.

For example, if you are an independent travel adviser who loves the snow, you could not only target travel magazines with new and interesting ski destinations, but you could also target local alpine radio stations or car magazines with advice on how to safely drive on snow-covered roads. Alternatively, you could pitch a press release detailing which ski resorts have the best childcare facilities to morning TV shows aimed at stay-at-home mums.

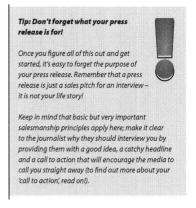

Tip: Don't forget what your press release is for!

Once you figure all of this out and get started, it's easy to forget the purpose of your press release. Remember that a press release is just a sales pitch for an interview – it is not your life story!

Keep in mind that basic but very important salesmanship principles apply here; make it clear to the journalist why they should interview you by providing them with a good idea, a catchy headline and a call to action that will encourage the media to call you straight away (to find out more about your 'call to action', read on!).

So how do I write a press release?

Ok. So now you've done your research, and thought

hard about content that interests your readers. You have your hook, and you know what niche media you're going to target. It's now time to nail the nitty-gritty of putting 'pen to paper' and write the press release that will sell you as a reputable and trustworthy expert.

Here in this section, I will run you through the basics of writing a winning press release. The two most important things to consider once you start to write are:

1. composition
2. and format.

I will explain them each in detail to show you what I mean.

It's incredibly important to stick to these techniques and rules. You want someone to pick up your press release and take it seriously, so it must look professional. Remember, you want to give the journalist the impression that you know what you're doing. You want them to think that you've played this game before, you're experienced, and you can provide fantastic interviews. They'll be more likely to call you because they'll think you're a professional, which makes their job a lot easier!

1. *Composing your press release*

When it comes to composing the content of your press release, stick to these rules, in order.

> If you read these rules and still aren't quite sure, there is an example of a well-composed and well-formatted press release at the end of this section for you to examine.

There is always a specific way that your content should be presented, and it involves the following four major parts:

01. Opening summary

Your opening summary starts your press release and tells people that you have something new and interesting to say. Touch on the topic by giving your reader information on what your press release is all about.

02. Quotations

Include quotes from yourself about the topic you have chosen. You may also want to include any other quotes that you can collect from other industry professionals that relate to what you have to say.

03. Credentials

In your press release, you need to convince the journalist why you're worth their time. To do this, give them your credentials so they know you are a credible and legitimate source of information. Include the details of any media coverage you may have received in the past. If you don't have any, start by telling the journalist how many subscribers, Twitter followers or Facebook fans you have. If you have written any e-books related to your business, you can include their titles in your press release as well.

04. Call to action

Motivate the journalist to take action when they read your press release by making it clear that you're happy to be interviewed. Remember, the purpose of your press release is to get this interview. You should be thinking of your press release as a sales letter. Sell your knowledge and expertise as an interviewee, and at the end of your press release write something like: "For more information call *[insert contact details here]*" or "Interviews are available with *[insert contact details here]*".

2. Formatting your press release

The format of your press release is extremely important, as this is what makes the first impression. As soon as the journalist receives your press release, they will give it a once-over. And if they notice any discrepancies that look unprofessional, they'll more than likely ignore it – or throw it away.

For the best chance of getting your press release read in detail, make sure you follow these formatting guidelines. They are: length, appearance, spacing, font and layout. Pay close attention as we go through each one in turn.

01. Length

Your press release should NEVER be more than one page long. If it takes two pages to tell your story, you're giving away too much information or you simply don't know how to tell your story in a short, sharp way.

Remember that the aim of your press release is to generate enough interest to score yourself an interview. By giving away too much information, the journalist has no reason to contact you, and they will publish the press release as is. Although this is better than nothing, you want them to actually call you for more information, and to make the feature article more interesting.

Alternatively, if you're blabbing too much in your press release, the journalist will see that you have bad communication skills, and think you're a bad interviewee. Why would they bother contacting you if they think you'll make their more job difficult or tiresome? Be as succinct as you can and always stick to the rule: your press release should only ever be one A4 page, and one A4 page only.

02. Appearance

Equally important is the overall appearance of your press release. Never write "Attention!" or incorporate gimmicks into your press release, hoping it will get a better response. You need to convey that you are a professional, an authority, an expert – not a salesman. Never deviate from the standard appearance of a press release; you may think it's cute or original and will help you get noticed, but it will not work and it will be rejected.

The standard press release is always printed in black ink on a single sheet of white paper. Do not use different coloured paper or ink – you'll look like an amateur. Likewise, don't throw in photos or any form of clip art. Such ideas may have previously worked in the movies but not in the real world. If you want to use attention-seeking tactics, use them for direct mail to connect with other audiences, not in press releases directed at journalists.

03. Spacing

Remember when you were at school, and your teachers always told you to submit work that was 'double spaced'? Well, they had a good reason. Not only is a well-spaced document is much easier to read, but it's also easier to jot down notes on (and that is why I have double-spaced this book!). There is more room for the journalist to write comments in areas of interest, which all contributes to a more cohesive and exciting article. So when formatting your press release, set the spacing on your computer at either 1.5 or 2.

04. Font

Once again, don't deviate from the standard format of a press release. It won't grant you that extra attention, it will just detract from the value of what you're saying. Stick with one of only two conventional fonts: Times New Roman or Arial. These are the only acceptable professional fonts that you should use at all times.

In addition, functions such as bold, italics or underline should be used sparingly. The only thing that should be bold in your press release is the headline. If you really feel the need to use italics or underline in the rest of your press release, then you may do so wherever appropriate – but try not to go overboard.

05. Layout

This is crucial. The layout of your content must look professional, and to do this, it must be done exactly the following way.

The top left hand corner must communicate the date of your press release. It tells the journalist when they can use the press release, and more often than not reads as follows:

FOR IMMEDIATE RELEASE

If your press release says 'for immediate release', this indicates to the journalist that your press release can be used anytime – is not restricted or linked to a time-sensitive event.

However, if you need to relay the message that your press release IS time-sensitive, then you must be specific. For example, if you need to push a story related to Valentine's Day, then you must write:

FOR RELEASE ON OR BEFORE VALENTINE'S DAY

Likewise, if there is a specific event that you are relating to, mark the date so the journalist knows:

FOR RELEASE BETWEEN 15 MAY & 20 MAY 2010

Although you're restricting potential publicity to a certain timeframe, promoting a time-sensitive press release does have its advantages. It helps you get noticed – the media is alerted to its time-sensitive nature and hence prioritise your press release over others. For this reason, time-checking your press releases often increases your chances of getting published.

Now to the top right hand corner. The top right hand corner is where you always place your contact information. It should always be formatted as follows:

FOR FURTHER INFORMATION CONTACT:
<insert your contact details or the contact details of a real person>

Note here that I've written 'the contact details of a real person'. Never use a company name, department or organisation. It's important that you always state the details of a real person because the journalist should be able to call and connect with someone directly, without having to work to find them. If the journalist sees they have to search for the contact person themselves, they will automatically discard your press release. They are very, very busy people and don't have time for such things. Make their job easier and ensure you have the phone number of a real person that they can get in touch with quickly and efficiently.

It's worth noting here that you could be sending out a press release on behalf of someone else

– maybe a company or a group. If this is the case, make sure that you inform the company or the group in advance that you are sending the press release out for them. I have heard horror stories where journalists have contact people that are listed on press releases without their prior knowledge. How embarrassing and unprofessional! Needless to say, in such cases, the publicity doesn't go anywhere and the whole exercise becomes a waste of time for all those involved (except us… isn't it great we can learn from their mistakes?).

In addition, this might sound crazily obvious, but make sure the phone number you provide is valid and actually works. Why don't you even check it yourself just to be sure? Never quote a 1800 or 1300 number as the journalist will immediately see they won't be directed to a real person (once again, don't waste their time and make their job harder for them!). Make sure you quote a direct line; if the contact has an extension number, be sure to include it.

To recap, the top of your press release should always look like the following:

FOR IMMEDIATE RELEASE	FOR FURTHER INFORMATION CONTACT: <insert your contact details or the contact details of a real person>

In addition, make sure that the text in this top section (both the left hand and right hand corners) is formatted in slightly smaller font than the font size of the main body. Although the text in these two top corners is important, it does not need to be in a large font to grab attention. (This also helps you fit everything you need onto the one A4 page.)

Many people format their press release the more traditional way – one line down after another along the left hand side. It looks like this:

> PRESS RELEASE
>
> FOR IMMEDIATE RELEASE
>
> FOR FURTHER INFORMATION CONTACT:
>
> Peter Williams XX-XXXX-XXX

However, the problem with this format is that it does not leave you much space. The format I mentioned earlier (that uses both the top left and top right hand corners of the page) allows you to fit more content onto the one A4 page. When your font is size 12 and double spaced, you only get about 25 lines of text. You may as well make the most of it – so try to avoid this layout.

By following these top rules, you follow way that the media actually lay out their press releases. So if you can emulate this, your press release will appear much more professional. This means it is more likely to be taken seriously, and hence, more likely to be picked up by a journalist. And consequently, you'll be more to generate some great exposure.

21 YEAR OLD SELLS M.C.G. - FOR UNDER $500

A 21 year old sports fanatic and AFL member is now selling the MCG to the widespread public - in pieces. He is giving the public a chance to own a part of Australian Sporting History which is set to disappear after this years AFL Grand Final when the rest of the MCC Pavilion is set to be demolished.

Peter Williams, is giving sporting fanatics and the widespread public the opportunity to obtain framed sections of the MCC Crested Carpet that once lay in the Ponsford Stand.

"People are so passionate about Aussie Rules, Cricket and the MCG" states Williams. "I don't want to see a big part of our culture simply die. I want to give everyone the chance to have a piece of Australian history and sporting legacy hanging in their homes, bars and offices"

"This is a exceptional and unprecedented opportunity," Sports Memorabilia Specialist David Fenech of Frame-Mem Collectables said. "Collectors are frantic when it comes to celebrities autographs, this is one better. Athletes and celebrities can sign infinitely, whereas this specific carpet is limited and can never be reproduced...an opportunity to good to pass up"

In addition to the limited MCC Crested Carpet, Williams is offering a small quantity of the pieces framed in authentic timber that also was once located in the now demolished Ponsford Stand, which saw over 30 years of sporting excellence.

Those wanting to purchase their own certified authentic piece of the MCG should visit www.SportingLimitedEditions.com

Further media enquires to Peter Williams on XXXX XXX XXX

Tip:

As an example, take a look at this press release that I wrote when trying to generate publicity for my MCG project. You can see that I've included the four distinct segments to my press release as well as a catchy headline that reflects my hook. I have kept the press release short and sweet, and my call to action (asking the media to contact me) is clear.

You can also see the format that you should follow every time. It is plain and easy to read, with FOR IMMEDIATE RELEASE and my contact details clearly marked at the top of the page.

Remember that your press release is not an article. It is important that you keep it sharp and to the point. You want to make your press release short enough that they are intrigued to find out more information. If you write too many words, the journalist has no reason to contact you.

You might initially think that it's great if your press release is published straight away, but ideally, you want to be able to contribute further to what you've already written. You want the additional publicity so you can be interviewed and provide supporting quotes, expert advice, and first-hand experiences. You don't want your press release printed word for word because if your press release gets published, that's as far as it will go!

How to distribute the press release

If your business is already producing content to improve SEO rankings and create backlinks throughout your site, you're probably already familiar with how to distribute material.

However, what's important to learn here is that the way you distribute content for SEO and backlinks is not the same as the way you would distribute content for publicity in offline media. The two methods are different; if you want to generate publicity in offline media, you have to target to journalists in a much more professional manner. If you want to be taken seriously, this includes enlisting a quality PR distribution company to send out your press releases for you. Here are the details on how to get started.

Finding contact details

When you considered what to write in your press release, one of the first things you did was carefully think about your audience and research what they wanted to know. Now think about where they intend to get that information from. It is this niche media (the magazines, TV channels and radio stations) that your customers are interested in, and therefore these are the targets you should be sending your press releases to.

So where do you find the journalists responsible for getting your interview featured in the media? There are several places to search for journalists, with targets found both online and offline.

For the names of people you should be pitching your press release to, you need to do a bit of research and look in the publisher's column of niche magazines. You can do this by walking to your local news agent, scanning all the titles relevant to your niche, and then looking for the editor's or journalist's details highlighted in the publisher's column near the front of the magazine.

If you're sitting at a computer, you can also find these names and contact details on the magazine's website (if they have one). While you're at it, you can continue to look for even more titles online. Research other magazines on Google by typing in the keywords relevant to your niche, followed by the word 'magazine'. Thanks to Google, you can now search and find plenty of journals relevant to your industry easily and conveniently from your own desk.

However! It is important for you to understand that if you are a professional actively working in a particular niche, you must aim to become familiar with all leading information sources relevant in your field. For example, if you are in the interior design industry, you should already be watching all renovation shows on TV and reading as many design and architecture-based magazines and blogs as possible. If not, make sure you become a subscriber – you should be an expert on all information available in your niche. Staying updated and being an industry leader at all times will help you stand out as a professional up-to-date expert – a key to ongoing business success!

Sending out your press release

Once you've done the research and gotten the contact details of the people you want to send your press release to, it's time to send it out. You can send a hard copy direct to the journalist via fax or post, or you can email it straight to their inbox. Snail mail is not as popular these days, although it is great if you have a fancy press package you can use to catch the journalist's eye. Faxes tend to stand out more than email these days because journalists' inboxes are flooded with emails all the time; your press release could get lost amongst all the non-urgent messages on their screen. If for any reason you're worried about sending your press release through, take the extra time to call the journalist first and let them know that your press release is on its way. But remember not to take up too much of their time.

You then need to be patient. Give the journalist ample time to review your press release. If you don't hear from them within at couple of weeks, follow up to make sure they have received it. If you have a great hook and exciting content, be confident that it's all about persistence – journalists are very busy and are often hard to get a hold of, but eventually something will stick if you keep contacting them enough with something interesting to say.

One of the best hooks you can present to the media is something topical – a press release that is related to hot gossip or current affairs at the time. People like to hear about things that are in the news and that are relevant today. If you can find a way to tie in your expertise to a hot topic, you're guaranteed to generate publicity, especially amongst media forms that have a high turnover of stories such as nightly news, daily radio programs and newspapers.

Using a distribution company

Tip: Be conscientious of time!

Be wary if you are posting a topical press release related to current affairs via traditional mail. Although it is far nicer to receive a hard copy press release instead of email these days, normal post can take a few days (if not longer) to get to the recipient. If you are sending out a press release that is of time-value, you can't afford to lose those few days, so stick to using email to make sure that your press release stays as relevant and effective as possible.

Doing the research and distribution of your press release on your own is the cheap, easy and manageable way to do it. But, if you're looking to target a lot of people that you don't have the time to look for, you can save much time and effort by paying a distribution service to do the work for you.

Although PR companies charge fees to distribute your press release for you, you will be amazed at how investing that little bit of money can also give you more credibility in the eyes of a journalist. Even if you only have $200 in your marketing budget, you're best to go to someone who can save you valuable time and send your press release directly to a journalist's desk.

By employing the services of a distribution company, you instantly look like a professional media expert. As soon as they can see that your press release has been delivered by a reputable company such as AAP Medianet, editors and journalists will realise that you know what you're doing, meaning your press release is more likely to catch a journalist's attention and be picked up for an interview. You can also use this service to reach a particular target market, which may increase your chances of receiving a response, and ultimately, an interview.

Be careful – you get what you pay for

There are many free PR distribution companies operating that claim to help send out your press releases for you. In fact, you may already be one to send out your blogs, increasing backlinks throughout your website and improving your SEO rankings. Of course, businesses can see the benefits of using these free PR distribution companies because it saves them time while costing them practically no money.

However, be careful, because you often get what you pay for. Because of the incredible amount of SPAM and increase in junk circulating in people's inboxes, journalists tend to ignore emails unless they are from a reputable media agency, such as AAP Medianet. I recommend that you only distribute your press releases through a professional and trustworthy company. You may end up discovering that the media is more likely to open an email if it came from you personally than from an unknown company anyway.

Tip: Maximise what you get out of the opportunity!

To increase your chances of your press release getting picked up by the media, why don't you help the interviewer interview you? A simple way to do this is to provide the journalist with a set of well thought-out prepared questions along with an answer sheet.

This helps the interviewer craft the questions they want to ask, which is especially good for live radio interviews. Providing edgy and thought-provoking questions will keep the interview interesting and make it appear less staged – it will look as though the interviewer is playing devil's advocate when they are actually just reading from a sheet of paper you had written for them (the audience will never know!).

Because they're short of time, there's a big chance they will take up your interview questions verbatim, which means that you will be well prepared. You already know what questions they're going ask before you go in.

You can also craft your questions and answers in such as way that you're able to pitch your product the way you want to, almost like a sales pitch hidden within the interview, along with a call to action. Radio announcers and journalists are very busy, so by providing these questions you're actually saving them time and making their job a lot easier, while giving you control over how you promote your business.

You can take advantage of this opportunity to lead listeners in a certain direction. For example, you could say "Well, you can check out more information at my website," and offer a free download or report of some description. By offering something of value to their listeners for free, the journalist can help you promote your website by saying, "check out our your exclusive listener offer at their website: [insert your website here]."

Summary

Although the prospect of coming up with an interesting story, compiling a press release and pitching it to the media sounds scary, the process is easier than most people imagine. If you're able to invest some of your time towards conducting valuable research, all you need to do is find out what people want to know, discover where they look for this information, and then find the journalist who has the ability to get you involved.

Once you've managed to find the contact details you need, your objective is to get interviewed. You can forward your press release to the media yourself or through a PR distribution company. Either way, to maximise your chances of getting it picked up by the media, you should always make sure that you have a good hook – the content of your press release needs to offer something interesting and useful to its readers, and if possible, topical to what's currently going on. You need to then pitch yourself as a valuable interviewee, making it clear that you're available to be contacted with a 'call to action' at the end.

Successfully generating publicity to raise your public profile is all about good content and persistence in following up with journalists. Try to make the most of the opportunity to sell yourself by preparing a questions and answer sheet in advance. Once you score this exposure, getting even more is easy. You can promote the publicity you received on your blog and in your folio, and continue to get even more publicity from there, achieving expert status along the way.

For more tips and useful information, check out some other resources at the end of this book.

Next, you'll learn how to 'provide' the content. Read on!

HOW DO YOU GET YOUR PRESS RELEASE INTO THE HANDS OF THE JOURNALISTS?

Go to www.MediaStrategiesForInternetMarketers.com
Sign up and download
Going Analogue's Press Release Distribution Video
for FREE!

Press release? Check. Bio sheet? Check. Q&A sheet? Check. You've now learned all you need to know about writing a press release so that you can get noticed. The key to success now is distribution.

In this video, Pete tells you:

- How to send out the press release
- What sending options you have depending on your budget
- What his *recommended* and *tested* press release distribution services are

And much, much more!

PART THREE
Providing the Content

What does 'Providing the Content' mean?

So far, we've learnt that 'being' the content means we are the person getting interviewed by the media. 'Providing' the content, however, is different. In this case, you are the person who creates the whole content from start to finish – such as an article that gets published in the media practically word for word. Unlike the objective of a short, sharp press release, which is to get you an interview, the objective of getting an article published is to show off your expertise with your name and credentials clearly marked in the byline of the story.

Generating publicity by providing magazines with articles is a fantastic and sure-fire way to build a great reputation. Businesses who are published get more credibility than those who aren't, so this is a great self-promotion strategy you should learn and continue to use for the rest of your professional life.

When writing an article for the media, you're given the opportunity to showcase your knowledge and professional expertise. Successfully pitching your article to offline magazines and newspapers helps your business get attention by instantly awarding you with expert status. Getting your work published builds credibility and shows people that you know what you're talking about – you immediately become a respected and authoritative figure within your niche. If you keep your article interesting, full of useful information, you'll be surprised how many people will stop, take notice, and absorb the information you have presented to them. This increases the strength of your presence in the marketplace, and draws more traffic to your website.

How do I get started writing an article?

So if you're keen to provide the media with an article, where do you start? You're probably asking yourself, "Where should I get my content from?"

For anyone running a serious business, this should be easy! As a thriving business, you will already have this kind of content circulating waiting to be re-used.

Dig around for existing content from your blogs, newsletters, subscriber emails, and marketing brochures; you should be able to re-use any form of regular communication that you send out to your former and prospective customers.

Anyone committed to making their business a success should already have some marketing and communication structures in place – businesses can't survive without them.

Repurposing your existing content

In this section of *Media Strategies for Internet Marketers*, I will teach you how to write an article. But before we get into it, I must remind you how important it is that you should be gathering content from material you've already written – blog posts, newsletters, emails and brochures.

Remember, if you're in a serious business, you should have these resources at hand. You should never have to start creating new content from scratch. With this type of content already stored in your computer, all you need to do is repurpose the existing content to turn it into an interesting article for your audience.

Repurposing your existing content involves reusing what you already have. Tweak it and make slight edits, so that it is suitable for a offline publications, in particular newspapers and niche magazines..

This method of reusing and repurposing content is the perfect way to use material that already engages your audience. Pick and choose the blog posts that have generated the most comments. Feedback from your readers is the best way to figure out whether your article is interesting, and the kind of responses you have received will also help you pitch your articles to editors.

Needless to say, this way of creating articles saves you time and effort. Get the most mileage out of whatever you already have! If you can learn to leverage what you've already got, you don't have to do any extra work. Just provide content that you've already written, and your business will still continue to increase leads and revenue.

Starting from scratch

For those who are new to business, or just don't have many existing resources to reuse, it's time to get serious – get writing! For any business to survive and thrive, you should be regularly blogging, sending out newsletters, writing emails and setting up auto-responders as part of your marketing plan. Communicate and stay in touch with your prospective customers and existing clients as much as you can! Regular communication via blog or email is integral to any marketing strategy belonging to a business that wants to expand.

To get a good grasp on what's involved when providing the media with content, this section of *Media Strategies for Internet Marketers* will teach you…

- Where do magazines get their articles from?
- How will getting published in offline media benefit my business?
- How do I write an article?
- Where can I get it published?
- Who do I pitch my article to?

Who do I send my articles to?

There are many media outlets where you can get published both online and offline. Getting published online means you can submit your articles to niche websites, article directories, and contribute to blogs or newsletters run by other companies. Successfully getting published offline will help you reach out to a much broader audience via magazines and newspapers, covering both those who use the internet, and those who don't.

Keep in mind that you do not have to limit yourself to local media. Go ahead and reach for titles interstate and overseas. There are so many to choose from around the world that you could successfully pitch your articles to. Once you create or repurpose your article to suit their audience, they will probably appreciate your international perspective as a guest contributor. Even better, you can then promote the fact you have been internationally recognised and published!

Magazines

Magazines are looking for valuable, quality content all the time. You can check them out at your local news agency. At the store, you'll see that the magazines are separated into different categories. Head to your niche area and you should be able to find most of the titles you need to know.

You can also conduct a search for magazines on the internet. Web searching various niche terms along with 'magazine' is always a good start. Other helpful websites include:

- <www.magazines.com>
- magazine subscription sites such as <www.isubscribe.com.au>
- Yahoo Directories online.

Newspapers

Don't just search for magazines alone – pitch your articles to newspapers as well. Newspapers are a great media outlet to be published in. They often have large readerships, and because newspapers are generally printed everyday, they are always on the lookout for interesting content, even more so than magazines.

Trade Journals

Trade journals are magazines and publications that are specific to a particular industry or trade. Some examples include *The Australian Woodworker, Heli News, Hair Biz,* and *Nursing Review.*

Although they all have very specific audiences (which is perfect if you'd like to target a particular type of customer), trade journals do include content on a variety of related topics.

Niche websites and their newsletters

There are many online niche websites run by industry professionals that serve as important sources information. They are almost like fan sites, oriented towards people who are passionate about absorbing as much news and information in that niche as possible. For example, <www.wakeonline.com> is a niche website geared towards all things related to the sport of wakeboarding in Australia, sometimes reporting news from around the world. The site details up-to-date industry news and allows readers to interact by giving them the option of posting comments.

Similar to magazines, these websites are always interested in good content. The directors of these sites not only use the content to post up on their homepage, but also to send out to their subscribers via newsletters and emails as well.

Article directories online

To meet the growing demand of people searching for information online, the number of online article directories has rapidly multiplied over the past few years. These directories welcome submissions and house hundreds of interesting articles across a wide range of topics – some even paying you for your work. Some popular online article directories include:

- <www.suite101.com>
- <www.articlesbase.com>
- <www.articleonlinedirectory.com>
- <www.ezinearticles.com>
- <www.goarticles.com>

How do I get published in print media?

If you're a serious business owner, you should in fact be getting published somewhere online already. However, once again, although blogging and sending out newsletters are great ways to reach out to your audience, they all target one type of customer: the online user. If you want to increase traffic to your site, change your strategy. Target people offline through magazines and newspapers instead.

To make this happen you need to send your articles to print media companies. And although this might sound tricky, getting publicity in magazines is much easier than you think! Let me explain.

Yes, magazines want YOU!

The purpose of a magazine is to sell advertising, not to provide content. You may not know it, but the articles (and even news and reviews) in magazines are actually written to promote certain products and services.

By capturing the interest of passionate niche readers, advertisers are able to connect with their desired demographic and generate hot leads for their business. The catch is that this can't happen without any editorial, because if there are no stories within the magazine, nobody will want to buy it. Editors, whether they are managing online or offline media, need content because they use these articles as hooks to sell their magazines containing ads. To make them more appealing, editors must fill the pages with interesting content – articles that their audience will want to read.

If you submit a quality article to a magazine, you actually make the editor's job easier – you save them the time they would normally spend searching for content themselves. By contributing interesting and useful articles, you're really doing them a huge favour. For this reason, if you can provide editors with quality content, you're almost guaranteed to generate some kind of publicity. Remember, without any content, there would be no magazine to read; it would only be a glossy brochure full of advertisements that would never sell.

To find the niche magazines you want to target, you will need to search for relevant magazine titles online through Google, or head into your local news agency to see what's on the rack – it's pretty much the same way you would get started looking for media if you were writing a press release.

But! I'd like to emphasise again that if you're serious about being an expert and a leader in your field, you should already be familiar with and reading every single industry magazine related to your business available. I cannot stress enough how important it is that you should be absorbing as much information as you possibly can to know what's going on and stay on top of developments in your industry at all times.

Once you've found the magazines you want to target, check whether they accept contributions from other authors and freelance writers before you send anything. An easy way to check is to read the publisher's column (the section where they list all the people who work at the magazine) – it is usually near the front of the magazine. If they publish a list of names under a heading titled 'contributors', that indicates they accept work from others outside their team of staff.

Submission guidelines

To maximise the chances of your article being published, I strongly recommend that you check these guidelines out before submitting any work. Editors provide guidelines so that contributing writers can match the way the editors do things in-house. These guidelines may include rules on formatting, such as spacing and font, how many words they accept, what type of articles they publish and what they don't, the kind of style they prefer, and what other information they may require before considering something for print.

If you can follow the way they do things in-house, you save the editor even more time and hassle when it comes to editing, meaning that your article is much more likely to be picked up out of the pile for print!

If you want to maximise your chances of getting published, you should read them carefully. It shows that you are well prepared and conscientious, and will also save the magazine staff valuable editing time. You can usually find them online, or contact the editor and ask them to send a copy to you.

How do I find the submission guidelines?

Usually submission guidelines are posted online or available for download on a magazine's website – just look on the site for a tab called 'contribute', or 'submissions'.

If they are not online, all you need to do is contact the magazine staff and ask for a copy via email. This will also give you a great opportunity to introduce yourself and express your interest in contributing an article.

If you would like an example, take a look at this casual and friendly email that I sent to Canadian publication *Dreamscapes Travel & Lifestyle Magazine.*

Hi there Dreamscapes Travel & Lifestyle Magazine,

I was wondering if you are open to accepting contributions from freelance writers? I would love to write an article for your magazine. If you are interested, could you please send me a copy of your submission guidelines?

Yours sincerely,
Pete Williams
Preneur Marketing, Australia
<www.preneurmarketing.com>

The Editor of *Dreamscapes Travel & Lifestyle Magazine* then promptly replied with the following email:

> **Dear Pete,**
>
> Thank you for expressing interest in contributing editorially to DREAMSCAPES TRAVEL & LIFESTYLE MAGAZINE. A copy of our Writers' Guidelines is attached. These should answer all your questions.
>
> Regards, Donna Viera

If you have never seen what submission guidelines look like, take a look below. This is the document that was attached to the Editor's email.

Carefully note how the submission guidelines clearly state what the magazine is looking for, including:

- Types of submissions
- Topics of interest
- Word count
- Deadlines
- Pay rate

These guidelines for *Dreamscapes Travel & Lifestyle Magazine* are extremely comprehensive, and also include additional information to help you such as:

- Type of audience
- Writing style
- How to submit photographs
- How to invoice
- Other helpful inspiring ideas

WRITERS' GUIDELINES FOR
DREAMSCAPES TRAVEL & LIFESTYLE MAGAZINE

I am open to receiving a list of those subjects and destinations about which you would like to write. Once you have done so, there is no need to resubmit your list of travel editorial ideas as I capture them permanently in my e-mail program. All you need to do is update me on your travels from time to time.

I set up and maintain a Personal Travel Profile on every writer who sends in editorial ideas. So, always be sure to include your mailing address and telephone contacts when you do submit editorial ideas. Every time you send in an idea, I update your personal profile accordingly. When we do require an editorial on a particular destination, lodging or theme, I contact only those whose names come up in my search. At that point, each one is asked to provide more information on the focus his or her editorial will cover, or, if I have specific information, I will let each one know what focus or destination I want covered.

While I sincerely appreciate your eagerness to assist us, if I do request editorial for specific destinations, please don't reply offering an alternative destination or theme that does not meet our specific criteria.

Being a Canadian publication, we try to give preference to Canadian travel writers who can fulfill our editorial needs and deadlines however we certainly commission stories from American and International writers as well. I often find a local's in-depth knowledge and perspective of an American or international destination interesting.

WHAT DO WE PAY?
The question everyone asks. We pay 30 cents (Canadian) a word and nothing for accompanying photography, although we do give credits, of course. This payment covers use in the magazine itself as well as its appearance in the online version of *DREAMSCAPES TRAVEL & LIFESTYLE MAGAZINE* at dreamscapes.ca.

SUBMITTING EDITORIAL IDEAS
Our current Editorial Schedule is posted online for your convenience under Media Kit at dreamscapes.ca. Next year's editorial schedule is usually finalized and posted online by early October.

Feature editorials range from 450 to 1,200 words, so please do NOT submit editorial ideas that require lengthier discussion. If you insist on e-mailing the editorial to me on spec, that is fine however, other than letting you know that I received it, I will not correspond with you unless we decide to use it. And please don't ask me to critique it.

If you are submitting an editorial idea for a specific issue, please send it along for consideration at least two months prior to publication. For instance, we start planning and assigning editorial content for our February 2007 issue the first week of December 2006.

We accept travel editorials that have been published previously. Please indicate when and where any previously published editorial has run when you do submit such an editorial idea. We also accept editorials from freelance writers whose trips have been fully or partially subsidized.

As far as *DREAMSCAPES* editorials go, ideally the grade level writing for all editorials should be at or near Grade 12 level. MicroSoft Word performs a readability test on documents as part of its spelling/grammar check option. The Flesch Reading Ease score rates text on a 100-point scale; the higher the score, the easier it is to understand the editorial. Aim for a score between 60 and 70. (Hint: Assess a version of your editorial that eliminates all references to URLs or e-mail addresses as these are tabulated by the software program and greatly affect the readability score.)

I recently read something that resonated with me because it spoke to the type of writing that I think our target audience appreciates: "What I'd prefer, though I may be part of the minority: essays that give me a new understanding of how the fundamental machinery of my country (and the world) works, what this machinery excludes, and what other possibilities people are exploring. Writing beautifully while providing fundamental insights into the workings of daily political and cultural life that will change the way the reader sees the world is a huge challenge. If I had my way, I'd have you look at each issue and ask: 'how did this change the understanding that Canadians have of their world in a fundamental and lasting way?'"

A challenge? Definitely. Especially when we have advertisers to keep happy. However, I believe it is possible to achieve a balance and it is a good editorial objective for writers to keep in mind.

In closing on this topic, I have one litmus test when selecting writers. If a writer cannot differentiate between when to use "it's" versus "its", I'm not interested. It's a pet peeve and also very elementary. Anyone who even considers "its'" a word is banished from my directory forever!

WHAT KIND OF EDITORIALS ARE WE LOOKING FOR?
The name of our magazine pretty well sums it up: editorials that relate to travel and lifestyle. The travel theme is clear but what do we mean by "lifestyle"?

Lifestyle coverage should be a mirror on how our society is changing—how we take care of ourselves, how we relate to each other, what we eat, wear, do for fun. It is a broad field that includes health, fitness, medicine, food, fashion, leisure, human interest, automotive, gardening, homes, real estate, psychology, social affairs and science. It is not necessary that the topic be related to travel.

While we are interested in destination-specific travel editorials, when it comes to themed or lifestyle editorials, ideally, we prefer the editorial to feature more than one destination or travel idea. For instance, if we publish an editorial on family travel, we would choose one that covers a few family destinations rather than what one specific destination offers families.

So keep that in mind, whether you choose to submit your editorial ideas as a list of travel destinations or a list of lifestyle/themed editorials. For instance, under a soft-adventure or eco travel theme, you might list Belize (2008), Peru (2007), California (2004), Australia (2006). Under a spa theme, your list might include Belize (2004) and California (2008), as well as Las Vegas (2006), Grenada (2007). If you prefer to submit a list of destinations, then it would look like this:

- San Francisco, California (2008): spas, dining, wine-tasting tours, cycling, river-barging
- Budapest, Hungary (2007): spas, history, culture, shopping, river cruises
- Las Vegas (2006): spas, dining, entertainment, shopping, golf, casinos, "a list of hotels/resorts"

As far as destinations go, I don't need you to go into a long explanation about what you did and where you went. I only need a brief outline. Another thing that helps me is if you let me know when you experienced each destination by simply adding the year in brackets as I did above.

With so many writers from around the world submitting so many ideas, how do you get noticed? Timing helps. Always refer to our Editorial Schedule posted online (under Media Kit) to ensure that the topics you submit for immediate consideration relate to the "travel season." For instance, while I probably am not interested in an editorial on Grenada in March, April or May, it might catch my eye in July for September, October or November. Then, before you submit your ideas, review each one to see if it can be linked to an upcoming celebration or anniversary or historical fact that might make it a timely piece rather than merely a general interest topic that can run anytime. You can always make it into a general interest piece if the "time factor" doesn't suit our needs.

Here's another question you might ask yourself about each topic you submit: "Is there a Canadian connection? " It might be as simple as a personal experience, or meeting a Canadian who moved to a "dream" location in pursuit of a dream, or discovering facts that relate to your personal family or our Canadian history.

SUBMITTING COMMISSIONED EDITORIAL
I only work with writers who have e-mail access. You may attach the editorial as a MicroSoft Word document or include it as a cut and paste in your e-mail.

Please, please, please do NOT format any of your editorial submissions. Simply submit all editorial as a single-spaced document using Times 12 normal font in regular upper and lower case format—no bold or underline or centering or page/section breaks formatting is required. Only use italics when mentioning the names of books, ships or when a word or phrase appears in a language other than English. By submitting your editorials this way, you save me a lot of time reformatting them so our Art Director can open up all the documents and lay them out easily. I sincerely appreciate your attention to this particular request.

EDITORIAL DEADLINES
I ask that all deadlines for editorial submissions be respected. These deadlines have been chosen because of other deadlines and commitments and when they are not met, delays either result in editorial postponements or additional costs on our part so it's really important to meet the deadlines. If you are unable to meet an editorial deadline on a particular subject, perhaps you can offer a story on a topic which you can provide by the submission date or you can let me know which subsequent issue deadline you might be able to meet. Please don't wait until a week before to let me know it cannot be done!

WRITING STYLE AND SPECIFICS

As an experienced writer, you have your own style, however, I do have some preferences. Personal leisure travel is an emotional purchase so I like to see an approach that tugs at the reader's heartstrings and tempts the reader to ask for more information or to travel. While a third-party reporting approach is great for the trade media, travel guides and brochures where hard facts are necessary to get reams of information across to those who sell travel, our readers have to be motivated to pick up brochures or to call the travel agent. I also prefer articles written in the "active voice" as opposed to the "passive voice." It makes for more dynamic and interesting reading.

Whenever it makes sense, feel free to inject "personal quotes or interviews" with travel/ hospitality experts (be sure to spell names correctly and to use official titles when quoting) you meet along the way, especially when referring to new and upcoming travel trends in the area/country visited. Also, as much as possible, please write editorial on a first-person basis as our readers prefer to read about personal, affordable, out-of-the-way travel experiences rather than impersonal "guidebook" text.

Please follow rules and guidelines outlined in the *Canadian Press Stylebook*, the *Globe and Mail Stylebook* and the *CP Caps and Spelling*.

KNOW YOUR AUDIENCE

For the most part, our readers are well travelled and well read. Distributed in major Canadian markets as a supplement in The Globe and Mail, *DREAMSCAPES TRAVEL & LIFESTYLE MAGAZINE* is published eight times a year with an audited circulation of 112,500 copies per issue. In addition, each issue is featured on our website at dreamscapes.ca with a link to our e-magazine, where readers can view the issue in its entirety. *DREAMSCAPES* is also polly-bagged with *Travelweek*—the Canadian travel industry's most trusted source of information—and reaches 12,000 influential travel professionals across Canada. Special mailings are sent to an additional 2,500, for a total distribution of 127,000 copies per issue.

Here are some quick facts you should know about our readers:

- Average Household Income: $143,000
- Managers/Professionals/Executives: 59%
- Age 36 to 64: 76%
- Age 35+: 88%
- Female: 45%
- Male: 55%
- Total Readership: 275,000+

EDITORIAL HEADINGS AND SUBHEADINGS

As the writer of the article, you have a much deeper attachment to it than the editor or the publisher does. I encourage you to please give your editorial pieces a heading—an eye-catching one. I also like to see subheads throughout the story that are meaningful to encourage readership. Subheads help to feed the information in bite-size pieces without overwhelming the reader.

TRAVEL PLANNERS

This is a requirement for all. As an absolute minimum, the Travel Planner must include the exact name of the tourist board or travel supplier(s) mentioned together with their website and telephone number (preferably a toll-free line from Canada). As long as you do not exceed the assigned word count, the sidebar can also include other information such as:

- Airlines, wholesalers or tour operators that offer a package or service;
- "Insider's information" on special rates, freebies, etc.;
- Favourite places to eat, stay, see the natives, places to go shopping, hear music, etc.;
- Local tourist information, money exchange, cost of food, transportation, etc.;
- What to do at night;
- Health issues, visa/passport/vaccination requirements.

Travel Planners are always included in the word count assigned.

EDITORIAL BY LINES
Always let us know how you want your name to appear with each editorial you submit.

PHOTOS AND CAPTIONS
Many of you prefer to provide support images and we appreciate that. Our budget is limited so we do not pay for photo usage, however, we are happy to give credit in all instances. Always let me know if you are providing photos, and always, always, always include:

- How you wish your name to appear in the photo credit;
- Cutlines for every photo you include. Well-thought out cutlines are key to higher readership and, who best to provide them than the person who took the photo!

When you provide photos, please send us a selection of both horizontal and vertical hi-res images. Strong, vibrant colours are best. Again, photos should have emotional appeal. These guidelines apply whether you are sending your own images or sending images from a tourist office.

When you submit your editorial ideas, simply let me know if photos are available, but please do not e-mail (or mail) the photos to me until I ask for them. When I do ask for images, you have a few options:

- The preferred option is to submit low-res digital images to me for selection purposes only. Once I have made my selection, I let you know where to send the hi-res formats. These can either be e-mailed or, if they are too large to e-mail, they can be uploaded to our FTP site (you will need FTP software which you can purchase online at tucows.com for under US$50). If this is your preference, please let me know when you submit your low-res images and I will provide you with the IP, logon and password information.
- You can burn your hi-res images onto a CD and mail or courier it to my attention at the address listed below. We do not return CDs as we assume that you have your original files.
- If a tourist board is supplying images that can be downloaded, simply provide me with the link and any download password info and I'm happy to do it at this end. If you have specific images that you think work best, please let me know.

WHERE DO YOU SEND EDITORIAL AND PHOTOS?
Please forward all editorials and digital images (preferably by e-mail or ftp) to:

Donna S. Vieira
Editor, *DREAMSCAPES TRAVEL & LIFESTYLE MAGAZINE*
642 Simcoe Street, S.S. #1
Niagara-on-the-Lake, Ontario L0S 1J0
E-mail: editor @dreamscapes.ca (primary); vnv@sympatico.ca (secondary)
Tel: (905) 468-4021
Fax: (905) 468-2382

MORE IMPORTANTLY, WHERE DO YOU SEND INVOICES?
Please note that you are responsible for invoicing. No invoice, no payment.
DREAMSCAPES pays for articles once the articles have appeared in an issue. In the
event we pull an assigned article, with no intentions of publishing it in a subsequent
issue, we pay a "kill fee" equal to 50 per cent. However, if the assigned article is not
published because it does not meet our editorial briefing or our editorial standards,
DREAMSCAPES does not pay a kill fee.

We do not pay for photos but we do give photo credits. If you do charge GST, please
ensure your GST number is included on your invoice. **Please do not send your
invoices to me as it only delays the payment process.** Please forward (faxes or
e-mails are acceptable) all invoices to:

Mr. Joe Turkel
Group Publisher
GlobElite Travel Marketing Inc.
3 Bluffwood Drive
Toronto, Ontario M2H 3L4
E-mail: dreamscapesmagazine@rogers.com
Tel: (416) 497-5353
Fax: (416) 497-0871

Your invoice should clearly outline which article and issue it covers and the length of the
article you submitted.

I trust these guidelines help you in your dealings with *DREAMSCAPES*. Should you
have any questions, please feel free to contact me. In the meantime, thank you for your
ongoing support and interest in contributing editorially to *DREAMSCAPES*.

Regards,
Donna S. Vieira
Editor, DREAMSCAPES TRAVEL & LIFESTYLE MAGAZINE

INSPIRATIONAL WORDS:
"Close the door. Write with no one looking over your shoulder. Don't try to figure out
what other people want to hear from you; figure out what you have to say. It's the one
and only thing you have to offer." — Author, Barbara Kingsolver

"My purpose is to entertain myself first and other people secondly." — Writer, John D. MacDonald

EXERCISE: Read something you've written recently, preferably something you're pleased with, or proud of, and see how the opening sentence reads. Are you moved by it, does it hook you in and compel you to read the next sentence, or make you want to read the whole book? Or have you delayed everything by describing the weather, or a conversation between two people? A powerful opening sentence can carry both the reader and the writer through an entire novel. Remember: We all have to wrestle with the muse and sometimes she lets us win. — Author, Bill Brooks

Here is another example of submission guidelines from *Quarterly Access*, a publication from the Australian Institute of International Affairs. These guidelines are not as detailed as those for *Dreamscapes Travel & Lifestyle Magazine,* however, if you ever have any questions that are not answered in the document, simply email them. Editors are generally very accommodating and are willing to help you with any queries you may have.

Quarterly Access Submission Guidelines and Important Notice to Authors:

A. **Important notice on submitting your work to *Quarterly Access***

We welcome unsolicited, previously unpublished submissions, if the content fits the quality standards, style and purpose of *Quarterly Access*. We especially welcome submissions by young, unpublished authors who wish to write for an intelligent, engaged audience of their peers.

Inclusion is entirely at the discretion of the editor-in-chief. By submitting any articles, stories or creative work to us you warrant that, apart from properly referenced quotations, your submission is your own work and contains no plagiarism. By submitting to us you also warrant that publication by us will not contravene the rights of any third party and that your submission is not defamatory. You also acknowledge that the editor-in-chief or his/her nominee may edit and amend your submissions before publication and by submitting you also give us licence to publish the submission in *Quarterly Access* and on the AIIA/ACCESS websites.

As a not-for-profit publication we are unable to pay contributors for their work.

Please e-mail your work in rtf, doc, or txt format to **quarterlyaccess@aiia.asn.au (please use as little formatting as possible)**

For inclusion in *Quarterly Access*, submission deadlines are as follows:
Summer 2011 issue: December 10
Autumn 2011 issue: March10

B. **Selection criteria**

Quarterly Access seeks to publish relevant and interesting articles that stimulate interest in and understanding of International Affairs. We seek to publish articles that display a high degree of intellectual rigour, and which expand debate in International Affairs.

C. **Types of material accepted for submission**

1. **Article (academic)**

   Authors have the opportunity to explore issues relating to international affairs in 2000-4000 words. Essays submitted should be original, engaging, topical, and written for a general audience of students and young professionals. Quarterly Access uses a footnote referencing style.

   We accept essays that were previously handed in for university assignments. However, we do not recommend that people do so without first substantially revamping them. The essays should be written appropriately for a general audience rather than an assessor, and in a clear, lively and engaging manner, while still displaying a high degree of intellectual rigour.

2. **Book Review (academic)**

   Authors have the opportunity to review a book relating to international affairs in 500-600 words. Quarterly Access uses a footnote referencing style.

3. **Interview (journalistic)**

   Quarterly Access seeks interviews with notable figures or people who have accomplished something out of the ordinary. Authors are encouraged to consult with the editorial team before conducting their interview by emailing **quarterlyaccess@aiia.asn.au**

4. **Travel Article (journalistic)**

   Quarterly Access seeks tales of adventure with insights relating to international affairs in 1000-2000 words. Past examples include a journey to Cape Town for the homeless world cup, or the challenges and rewards of development work in Sri Lanka. Authors are encouraged to provide photographic material to accompany their article.

5. **Feature Article (journalistic)**

   Quarterly Access seeks feature articles relating to international affairs in 1000-2000 words.

To submit your work email quarterlyaccess@aiia.asn.au

Adhere to guidelines and save yourself time

Obviously different publications have different submission guidelines. Memorise the submission guidelines for all the magazines relevant to your niche once you get to know them. Copy them, using the same style for all of your blog posts so that they look styled and professional.

If you can memorise and copy the submission guidelines for different magazine titles, match them to your own content! Apply these guidelines to whatever new content you create in the future. This means that your new blog posts will be ready to go if you choose to submit them for print, saving you time and effort because you won't need to change them again!

If you're too busy, get a ghostwriter to become familiar with these guidelines for you. They can then help you efficiently write and pitch your article in their house style, once again helping you get the most mileage (with minimal effort) out of whatever content you've got.

If you're not sure what you're doing, or you aren't a confident writer, or just don't have the time, consider hiring a ghostwriter to assist you! Sure, it may cost a little cash upfront to get the content written, but at least it will be professional. You'll save time and reap the financial rewards once your article gets published.

The benefits of getting your article published

The Halo Effect (yes, it's back again!)

Just like scoring an interview in the media, getting an article published in a magazine also has a huge positive effect on your reputation. This exposure awards you with that 'Halo Effect' we talked about earlier in Part Two of this book (pages 17-18).

The 'Halo Effect' is one of the most important tools you can use to help promote your business. If you can become published in a magazine or newspaper, your business builds credibility and a trustworthy relationship with potential customers.

What's more is that once you have become published, keep track of where you've been featured. You can then

Tip: Hire a ghostwriter!

If writing is really not your thing, collaborate with another writer to get the job done.

Ghostwriters can help you create new content or repurpose any existing content that you already have. If you don't know any ghostwriters that can help you, simply Google search terms like 'ghostwriters' or 'freelance writers'. If you prefer a writer near you, you can also specify the area you live in or work from.

However, there are plenty of good writers all over the world who can help you out! Some great websites to look through include <www.freelancer.com>, <www.odesk.com> and <www.ozlance.com>.

Remember that getting published offline should be an easy task – something that does not require extra work. Employing a writer helps you do this – they complete the job quickly, easily and professionally and save you lots of time.

collect a copy of all the affiliated logos and post them on your website. You can also highlight the logos of where you've been published in your newsletters and emails.

By being able to say "As seen in…", you're instantly granted expert status, and at the end of the day, this is guaranteed to help you increase your conversion rate!

Marketing to buyers who are already interested

Another benefit to getting an article published in print media is that magazine readers are one of the best audiences to target. People who subscribe to magazines are already buyers – they are willing to hand over their cash to absorb more information about their niche. Your chances of converting them into hard sales are much higher because you already know they are willing to spend money on something that interests them (after all, they bought the magazine in the first place). On the other hand, online users who search for information via Google are less likely to be converted into sales because they are usually looking for free information.

If you think that your article is suitable for more than one magazine, feel free to pitch it to different titles unless the editor of a magazine specifically asks for exclusivity/sole rights to your work. If you can get published across a range of several magazines, you will reach out to even more readers. What's even better is that you can then promote the fact you've been featured in several different titles, positively adding to your public profile.

Your byline or author's box

This byline, or author's box, comprises just a few lines that describe who you are, what you do, and what your credentials are. It shows the reader your expertise and experience, and helps explain why you are authorised to write about that particular subject. This is often also where people see your contact details.

This byline, along with quality content, is one of the keys to increasing sales; it helps direct people to your website. Make it clear that keen magazine readers can check out your website for more valuable information. The credibility that you have established in the media will dramatically increase your conversion rate once they visit if they're looking to buy.

When you submit your article, it's often up to you to write your own byline that clearly states your name and your credentials. This is your chance to toot your own horn; write a positive two-line description of what you and your business do best.

Most importantly, however, make sure you include a call to action with your byline. Although you should have already added a call to action within the conclusion of your article (more on that later), there is no harm in reinforcing the idea that readers can find more information and

HOW DO YOU ENSURE THAT YOUR CONTACT DETAILS ARE PUT IN THE ARTICLE?

Go to www.MediaStrategiesForInternetMarketers.com
Sign up and download
Unleashing the Power of Publicity's Dan Janal Interview
for FREE!

Dan Janal is an internationally recognized speaker, Internet marketer and best-selling author. As president of Janal Communications, he conducts strategic planning seminars and consultations for clients ranging for start-ups to Fortune 1000. Dan was on the PR team that launched America Online, the #1 online service, and personally directed the PR launch of Grolier's Electronic Encyclopedia, the first consumer software program ever produced on a CD-ROM.

In this video, Pete and Dan reveal...

- How publicitiy made AOL the world's largest ISP
- How to get journalists calling you for interviews
- How to deal with reporters successfully
- How to construct powerful releases

And much, much more!

special offers online. You want to encourage them to visit your website as much as you can, so don't forget to list the web address with your contact details!

The four steps to writing an article

So how do we go about generating the content that magazines need? Once again, the first thing you need to do is take a look at what you've already got. Keep in mind that it's all about using what you have, not creating new stuff.

Your business is probably already producing valuable blog posts, newsletters, auto-responder sequences, and e-zine articles. Now it's just a matter of leveraging that existing content by repurposing your work. Make the most out of the resources you already have; this is the same kind of content magazines want.

But if your article doesn't already exist, you'll have to write one. For those who need help starting from scratch, there are four parts to writing your own article.

1. Figuring out what to write

Know your niche

It's really important that you should already know exactly what you want to write about. You should be an expert and well-versed in your niche. You should know a lot about this subject and have specialist skills previously developed from your professional experience.

To maintain your knowledge, you also should be continually engrossing yourself in industry newspapers and journals, and researching as much as you can that's relevant to your field. Stay updated with what's going on, be aware of what changes are happening in your niche, and what might happen to your industry in the future.

It's crucial that you acknowledge that you should be scripting everything you know about your subject to successfully run your business and stay on top of your game, not just for backlinks, SEO or to get published in the media. Do this – absorb yourself in your niche – for the sake of your business.

If you need a little push in the right direction, think about the broad category that you specialise in and what you're good at. The subject you choose for your article could be based on life experiences and lessons that you've learnt either at home or at work, or it could also be something you happen to know a lot about because you are passionate about that subject. Either way, remember to stick to what you know well, so you can position yourself as an expert in that particular niche.

Doing your research

Just like with a press release, you're going to have to investigate into what people want to read about. Choosing a subject to write about requires just as much research as trying to come up with good content for a press release, if not more. To revisit how to research your audience, pretend you are the consumer. What would you want to know? You need to provide them with content that they will be inspired to read by figuring out what type of information they are looking for.

Remember, in Part Two of this book, we covered several ways to conduct research. To refresh your memory, here is a quick run down (or you can re-read pages 20-22).

If you are a serious business owner, you should have an email list consisting of former customers and subscribers. Take advantage of this resource and email them questions to find out what they want to know. You could also distribute hard copy surveys, or create electronic questionnaires and send them out via email or Survey Monkey.

Scoping out what people are asking each other online is another great way to find out what people want to read about. Google-search niche community forums, read industry blogs and research what comments are being posted up online.

Don't forget to also visit the Yahoo Answers website – it is a treasure trove of ideas and information. Users from all around the world use Yahoo Answers to ask each other questions about real life topics over the internet – these are exactly the types of questions and topics that people want to read about!

Take advantage of this resource. Yahoo Answers gives you the perfect opportunity to answer these questions for them with well-written professional advice. Furthermore, rest assured that whatever topic you find via Yahoo Answers will be published; magazines will want to print articles on these topics because it is precisely what their audiences want.

Lastly, keep your finger on the pulse easily with Google Alerts. Google Alerts monitors specific search terms and sends email notifications on your chosen topic directly to your inbox for you. All you need to do is sign up. You don't need to worry about finding those extra hours to conduct research – the news comes to you. Best of all, it's free!

Picking a topic within your niche

Once you have identified what subject you are going you write about, you need to narrow this down to a more specific topic. Subjects themselves are very broad so you need to pick a particular aspect of that subject. To do this, focus on what your subject of expertise is, and then refine your article to feature just one small part of that subject of expertise. If you were to write an article about a subject without refining it, you could end up writing thousands of words forever!

Apart from the fact that long articles are boring, it's standard for most articles to range between 500 and 2000 words depending on the publication (these details can vary, but you can check this information in the magazine's submission guidelines). You'll definitely need to narrow down the topic of your article to maintain the reader's interest – it's easily digested and more entertaining that way. If your article stays within this healthy word count, it becomes more manageable and enjoyable to read.

If you're not quite sure what I mean, here is an example of refining a broad subject into a narrow topic:

> **Waterports > Waterskiing > Waterski Equipment >
> "The Latest Technology in Waterski Equipment"**

You can see here that I've picked the broad subject of watersports, and refined the idea down to one aspect of this niche. But where possible, try to make your article topical and relative to what's hot in the news. If you can create an article that's in line with what everyone is currently talking about, your story becomes more valuable and is more likely to be picked up by the media. A topical example:

> **Waterports > Waterskiing > Waterski Equipment >
> "Which Waterski Brands Won The Most Medals at this
> Summer's World Championships?"**

Address your audience's interests

Another important factor you should consider when deciding what to write about is the objective of your article (other than directing readers to your website, of course!). Are you offering readers new information? Are you out to persuade them with your research? Are you revealing observations related to a recent investigation? Are you out to discover, teach, or simply express your opinion? You could talk about something new, and encourage people to think outside the square by offering insight or commentary that is unusual and different.

Think about the motivation behind the content you choose for your article. It will help if you can think about how you want your audience to feel. Some useful questions to think about are: "What is it that they want to know or learn that relates to that particular subject?" or "Can I help them by addressing common queries and offering them valuable advice?"

Once you've thought about your topic, ask yourself: "What's the style of my article?" Informative stories, such as 'How To' articles are some of the most common articles that businesses write. They're often very successful because it shows that businesses are able to identify concerns that their prospective customers have, and provide them with solutions in the articles they present.

Figuring out what questions people are asking each other is key to providing your audience with something interesting, useful and new. Once you get thinking, you'll realise that all these questions sound familiar – they are all the same questions that you once wanted to know before you became an expert in your niche.

Engage your audience with your words

One of the most crucial questions you should ask yourself is: "Who is reading my article?" When putting your article together, you must consider what your audience would be interested in and understand them; more specifically who they are, how old they are, are they male or female, how much money do they make and what kind of lifestyle do they have?

The type of audience and publication you want to target will affect the tone of voice you use throughout your article. There are no general rules – it can be casual or it can be formal – other than the fact that it should connect with your audience in the right way.

Also, you should figure out how much your readers will already know about your particular topic so that you can tailor your article to suit them. For example, people who read waterski magazines will probably already know a lot of basic information about waterski equipment. But people who read boating magazines might not know anything about waterski equipment, however may still have an interest in waterskiing. Make sure you pick content that is appropriate, and then go into the right level of detail accordingly.

2. Creating an attention grabbing title

Just like creating a headline for a press release, the headline of your article should catch the interest of your reader straight away. You need to make sure that you motivate your reader to find out more.

A good way to seize someone's attention is to create a headline that offers the reader help. Make it clear in the headline that your article will teach them something useful that they'll be able to take away with them after reading and apply in their professional or personal lives (this is why informative and instructive "How To" articles work so well!).

Something to keep in mind when creating your headline is to make sure you use keywords in your title. This will help clarify exactly what your article is about, and be more easily picked up by people who have an interest in that topic. Using keywords in your headline also helps especially if your article is published online as it improves your SEO rankings. But don't forget, you should be aiming to generate publicity offline as well as online to really get the best results out of your marketing efforts.

Depending on what type of article you're writing, here are some common examples that might help you get started:

- If you're offering advice, open your headline with "How To..." or "The Best Way To..."
- If you're giving readers new information, open your headline with "Studies Show..." or "New Research Reveals..."
- If you're offering a solution to a reader's problem, open your headline with "Do You Suffer From...?" or "How To Beat..."
- Your article might inspire the reader with insight and curiosity, so open your headline with "What Do ... and ... Have in Common?" or "The Biggest Myths About..."

3. Writing your article

The Introduction

The introduction of your article is the opening of your story. It introduces what you are going to write about in just one or two short paragraphs. In conjunction with your catchy headline, your introduction is supposed to persuade the reader to keep reading. It expands and reflects on the headline that you have provided, offering readers insight to what they are about to learn, without divulging all the information straight away.

The introduction also explains to your audience why the information you are about to present is important and why it is relevant. This helps the reader establish why they are bothering to read your article. Busy readers are often asking themselves, "What's in it for me?" – it is assurance that they are going to get something out of it once they're finished.

The Body

The body is the heart of your article, where you expand on your argument and present all the information relevant to your topic. Throughout the body of your article, try to stick to short paragraphs about two or three sentences long. You'll find that your points will read a lot clearer, making your article much easier to follow. (Besides, big chunks of writing turn people off from reading straight away!)

Another way to break up your article into an easy-to-understand structure is to use subheadings. These are small titles throughout the body of your text that work to introduce the next block of text. Make your subheadings bold so they stand out. Subheadings separate your article into clear sections, making it even more manageable for the reader to understand. Subheadings are also great for maintaining a reader's attention because the article becomes easier to scan and follow.

To make the body of your article even more interesting, add pictures throughout (or in addition to) your article. These can be images, or tables or diagrams that detail core information. This helps to keep your article visually interesting and often more convincing, while still presenting the information you need to complete your story.

When writing the body of your article, remember to keep your text simple, easy to read and as relevant to your topic as possible. Try to incorporate as many keywords as you can, without making it sound unnatural and repetitive. These keywords reinforce to the reader that the article is about a topic that interests them. And although you should be branching out to magazines and newspapers to reach offline prospects, once again, using keywords helps especially for online articles – they become easier to find on search engine pages, and the more keywords you use, the higher your page ranks on Google.

The Conclusion

Once you have made all the points that you want to present throughout the body of your article, you have to summarise what you've written. Your conclusion is a summary that helps your readers remember the purpose of your story. It may have been a self-help article, or an exciting piece that reveals new and intriguing findings. Either way, you do not need to go into unnecessary detail – just touch on the central theme of your article to remind readers what useful information they should take away from it (i.e. how they can apply what they've learnt in your article in their professional or personal lives).

Your summary should be short and simple. Depending on the overall length of your article, aim to keep your conclusion just one paragraph long (maybe two or three at the most). It is important that you don't introduce anything new to your article here – everything that you want to discuss should already have been written within the main body of your article.

It is important to remember that the purpose of your article is to drive people to your website. So, similar to a press release, you want to include a clear call to action.

Make sure that your conclusion encourages readers to visit your website by telling them that they'll be able to find more information online. Although you want to pack your article full of interesting hints and tips, you want to lure them to your site. Only share enough information that drums up interest or teaches them the fundamentals of what they'd like to know. If you can keep some details to yourself, you give your readers a reason to get in touch with you.

You can also encourage them to visit your website by offering exclusive discounts for readers who register their details online (yes that's right, you should be compiling subscriber lists all the time!). Most importantly, end on a positive note. You want to inspire your readers, not get them down.

Proofreading and revision

Article writing doesn't end once you've written your conclusion! It is a challenging process that requires many revisions to get right. Your article may not be perfect the first time around. Once you've completed a first draft, you will need to revisit the article so you can clearly see whether it reads well and whether or not you are happy with it.

Go back through your article and ensure that all of your spelling and grammar is correct and consistent. If you're using a program such as Microsoft Word, it's important that you don't rely on spellcheckers. Automated spell-checkers often miss grammatical mistakes that only you'll be able to pick up (i.e. the difference between 'there' and 'their').

It is usually takes at least one day for you to see any mistakes, so make sure you set aside the time to step away from the computer and revisit your article again with fresh eyes. Proofreading is your opportunity to check that everything you have written makes sense. Once you take another look at the words you have put together, your brain can analyse whether your article can be improved, and if so, how. See whether you can reword your article to make it say what you want to say more clearly, or more accurately.

It always helps if your friends and family can read your article too. Their honest and constructive feedback will help you gain a better understanding of how it can be improved before you submit it to any journalists.

4. Getting it published

Make sure you provide something of interest to your audience

Getting your article published can sound tricky but don't be afraid to pitch it to the media. To get your article picked up, you just need to show them that you have something worthy to say that positively contributes to their reader's interest. (This is why you should have done your research well in advance to find out what people want to know!)

Tip: Another reason to reuse existing content!

A huge part of this book has been reiterating that you should be repurposing what you already have to create content. The proofreading and revision stage serves as another fantastic reason for this. Allow me to explain...

If you have already published a blog post online or sent out a newsletter to your subscribers, chances are that you have also generated some feedback from it.

If you can repurpose content that others have already read, take advantage of the comments that people have written! Essentially, anyone who has provided feedback has helped proofread it for you - they will have stated their opinion on the topic, point out what they think is correct and incorrect, and tell you things that you may have missed out.

This adds another dimension to the proofreading stage. It gives you the perfect opportunity to reflect upon any comments and suggestions, and use the discussion to improve your article even further before sending it off for print!

Once again, I can't stress enough that there is no point pitching your article to a magazine that has nothing to do with your topic. Maximise your chances of being published by only submitting articles to relevant publications that have readers who will be interested in what you have to say.

To help you do this, get to know the publication before you send off a submission to make sure it fits in with their demographic. You can purchase back issues to familiarise yourself with them, or read up about them if they have a website online.

If you article does not relate to the particular magazine, all you need to do is tweak it slightly with a fresh new angle so that is becomes relevant to that niche. If not, you waste your time (and theirs!), and the editors will not be interested in hearing from you again.

> **Tip: Tweak and repurpose content!**
>
> If an editor says no to publishing one of your articles that has already been featured elsewhere, ask them if they would be happy for you to rewrite it with a slightly new angle. You don't have to do much work to change it, just tweak it to make it more suitable for their audience. Repurposing your own work that has already been published is a great way to leverage off what you've already written, without having to go through the effort of starting all over again.

Pitching your article to the media – how to get started

If you haven't received any publicity before, you have to start small. Smaller publications and websites are more likely to publish your content, and may even help you along by giving you constructive advice before they publish it for you.

I would suggest starting out with a local newspaper or magazine. Once you become published, collect these press clippings and compile a portfolio for yourself and your business. It might be neat to look at and show off to your friends, but more importantly, your folio is the perfect tool to help you generate even more publicity. As your folio grows, so does your reputation and credibility, and before you know it, you'll be able to contact bigger media companies with good chances of them picking up and publishing your article.

Query letters

When you pitch your article to the media, you do not send them your whole article. Instead, you send them a friendly letter or email, known as a 'query', that showcases your headline, a short synopsis of your article, an explanation of why it's interesting and why you're experienced enough to talk about it.

I strongly recommend that you keep your query letter short, simple and easy to read. Try to stay away from bright colours and designs – you might think it is more likely to attract a journalist's attention, but it looks unprofessional and trust me, they know good content when they see it. There is no need to waste your time and effort trying to make it look fancy.

Also, remember that you should only send query letters to magazines suited to what you've written. There's no point in pitching articles that don't have anything to do with the magazine's readers, so make sure that your content interests their audience. If you need to tweak your article to make it more appealing to slightly different readers, go for it!

If you're still not sure, of haven't seen a query letter before, here is an example of a query letter that I have written for you:

DIY Painting

Dear XXXX,

I currently run a online website/blog focused on the DIY Home Improvement Market; primarily offering DIY Painting tips, tricks and articles - with over 130,000 unique readers every month.

A recent article I posted on my site about "How To Get 3 Times The Coat Coverage From a Typical Paint Can" has been extremely popular with over 300 comments and replies.

The article talks about a little known trick that a 20 year painting veteran shared with me; and not only is the article educational; but the part about how he has only has one arm is hilarious.

I've been a long time reader of {Magazine Title}, and I believe the piece could be a perfect fit with your audience for an upcoming edition.

The piece is currently 853 words long (which I am happy to edit/expand) and I have some great hi-res photographs to go along with the article.

You can seethe article in its current form over at: http://www.PaintingIsNotHardWork.com/blog/

Thank you for your consideration, and I hope to hear from you soon.

Sincerely,
Pete Williams
Email
Phone
Address Line 1
Address Line 2

Make contact and follow up with the editor

After you send out your query letter, be patient. It is common to have to wait a reasonable amount of time before anyone gets back to you. Once several weeks have passed, follow up with the editor nicely over the phone. If they are too busy, try to send them a friendly email instead. Continue trying to get in touch with them, but be reasonable – you don't want to be obsessive about it and annoy them. Just be persistent.

Eventually, they'll make contact and get back to you. Ask them if they received your query, and what their honest opinion was. If they didn't like it, or didn't think it was appropriate for their readers, ask them how you could alter it to suit their audience better instead of taking no for an answer. You might find that a few minor changes is all that it takes to get the editor interested in printing your article.

If the editor declines your pitch entirely, it is important that you take away their feedback and suggestions – figure out what they like and don't like, so that you have a higher chance of getting published the next time you pitch to them again.

Other tools you can use to get attention

If you've never been publicised in the media before, it can be very difficult to get a journalist's attention. But there are ways around this. Just because you haven't had articles published before does not mean that you aren't worth listening to.

When pitching your story to a journalist, tell them not only your credentials, but also list how many Twitter followers or Facebook fans you have (as serious business owners, you should already have these social media tools in operation!). You can also include how many books or e-books you've written (if any).

Alternatively, if your article has already been published online in the form of a blog post, show off the number of page views you've had. You can also show off how many comments you've had, and even tell them how many times it's been 'tweeted' and 'retweeted' online.

Tip: Get featured regularly!

Once you have gotten in touch with the editor, maintaining contact with them is a great way to build a working relationship. If you can continue the working relationship, the editor can help tell you what type of content they are looking for next, and even assign particular articles to you on subjects they think you are an expert on.

Being regularly featured in the media is one of the best types of publicity you can get. It demonstrates that you are always on the pulse with the latest industry news, knowledge and expertise, and proves to other media outlets and prospective customers that you're not a one hit wonder and worth being profiled on a regular basis.

These are all great ways to convince the journalist that they're probably going to be interested in what you have to say. By proving to the journalist that you already have some kind of professional presence, you present the media with 'social proof' (yes, that's right – we've talked about this already!).

This social proof shows the media that you have fans and followers who like to read what you've got to say, sometimes even chipping into the conversation by posting comments online.

Journalists will think, "Wow, this guy must be interesting," and can rest assured that your article will generate attention and get people talking.

Tip: Work together!

If you're popular online (i.e. have lots of followers and page views to your website everyday), you can also tell the media that you can work together to cross-promote as a team. You can post comments and articles related to them on your website to help them generate more publicity and reach out to more people – it's a win-win situation.

PART FOUR
Conclusion

This is only the beginning...

Generating publicity in the media to increase your conversion rate is just the beginning of a successful marketing plan. There are so many opportunities out there to gain more exposure and boost your sales. What we've covered in *Media Strategies for Internet Marketers* only scratches the surface.

Using a list broker

As described in this book, there are plenty of ways to generate free publicity and attract people to your website without spending money on traditional advertising. One of the most effective is direct mail.

The key to finding buyers who can easily be converted into sales is to find specific lists of prospects within your niche. To find these lists, you can go through legitimate list brokers.

List brokers collect a wide spectrum of information based on whatever forms people consensually fill out. These can include boxes that viewers tick on websites for special offers, online or hard copy surveys, or magazine, newsletter or email subscriptions.

List brokers will be able to give you the names and details of the particular people you want to target – all you need to do is tell them your criteria. For example, you could specify that you'd like the names of all men aged 20-30 living in the south-eastern suburbs of Melbourne. Or, you could ask for the names of readers who subscribe to particular niche magazines – people who already take an interest in spending money on something they love.

This is one of the most effective ways to market your business. Rather than pitching your business to random prospects, list brokers help you target people who have already expressed a relative interest in your niche.

AdWords VS Direct Mail

If you're internet-savvy, you're probably already promoting your business using Google AdWords. Depending on your keywords and how many people click through to your ad, you could be paying anything from a few cents to a few dollars for every single click that goes to your page.

What's so surprising is that when you compare how much it costs for you to implement traditional direct marketing, it can actually work out to be a cheaper marketing option per person than using Google AdWords!

WHERE DO YOU FIND PEOPLE ACTIVELY LOOKING FOR YOUR PRODUCTS OFFLINE?

Go to www.MediaStrategiesForInternetMarketers.com
Sign up and download
Going Analogue's Buying Direct Mail Lists Session
for FREE!

No doubt you're very familiar with buying e-mail lists for your online marketing activities. Pete interviews an expert on how to do the same with physical addresses and why this can be so valuable.

In this interview, Pete talks about:

- How to buy a list
- What questions you should be asking when buying a list
- How you could sell your own list and rent it out to other people

And much, much more!

If you don't believe me, let me give you an example. For most businesses, the average cost of Google AdWords is 50 cents per click. Approximately only one in five people who click through to your site lead to a sale or opt in to your mailing list. This means that you're really paying around $2.50 for each hot prospect or subscription.

Now let's compare this to direct mail. If you engage the help of a list broker, you can often buy names for about 50 cents each — on par with the cost per click when using AdWords. But the difference is that these names will be specifically targeted to your niche. This means that you'll have a much higher chance of pulling through with a sale, giving you better delivery rates. This is far more effective return on investment, at only one fifth of the cost!

Summary

All businesses want to make money — grow, expand and survive in a competitive marketplace. To do this, businesses engage in marketing. But running a website for your business is not your only marketing strategy. Remember that you're running a real world business, not just a website. And because your business is a real world business, keep in mind that there are ways to successfully market your business that go beyond the internet.

To reach as many people as you can, 'go analogue' — engage in offline marketing and find prospects who do not ordinarily search for your products online.

In *MEDIA STRATEGIES FOR INTERNET MARKETERS*, we've taught you to do this either by sending in press releases or pitching interesting articles. Whether you choose to 'be' the content or 'provide' the content, your subsequent publicity will produce successful results.

By generating publicity in the media, you encourage more people to find out information about you and your business via your website. This generates more leads thanks to an increase in traffic to your site, and because you have been featured in the media, you are endowed with the 'Halo Effect'. By being given this form of 'social proof', consumers will trust you and are more likely to purchase from you once they've taken the action to check out your site online.

All of these factors result in increased visits to your site and consequently higher conversion rates overall.

The key point of this book, *MEDIA STRATEGIES FOR INTERNET MARKETERS*, is to teach you that although Search Engine Optimisation (SEO), Google AdWords and other forms of internet marketing are great marketing tools, they ARE NOT the only effective marketing tools available.

In addition to getting published in newspapers and magazines, there are many different ways you can generate effective leads, including postcard marketing, distributing targeted direct mail, and listings in classifieds. And although we may be living in a modern digital-based world, these traditional offline methods have worked for the past 50 to 100 years, and they will still continue to be profitable in the future.

The secret to business success is simply advertising where your prospects are!

And by now I hope you've discovered that they are not only online, but they are offline – reading these newspapers, opening the envelopes in their mailbox, listening to the radio and buying the magazine from the newsstands.

So if you're serious about taking your "online business" to the next level and are going to implement the techniques and strategies, GET STARTED TODAY!

Make a deal with yourself, set aside 45 minutes a week for the next four weeks (that's only three hours) to actually take action and test some of the methods that are now in your marketing arsenal.

And if you want some more help, support and in-depth training, you'll probably also want to check out www.GoingAnalogue.com.

So what's GoingAnalogue.com all about?

I'm going to take you through a programme of four modules spread over eight weeks and show you in step-by-step detail how I've exploited offline techniques to boost traffic to websites, to convert visitors more effectively and ultimately, to generate more revenue.

This online training course will NOT focus on the stuff we've already covered here, high-level strategy, fluffy concepts or leave you hanging with the 'how to' details. That's just not what I'm all about. We're going to go deeper than the typical 'why and what' that's covered in most online courses, and give you the clear 'how to' lessons – lessons on offline techniques beyond the press releases and article syndication covered in this book.

When you join us at GoingAnalogue.com, you'll instantly receive a series of step-by-step video guides, which link together to form a complete process for offline marketing for your online business. Each session will contain links to the resources you need and case studies on how I and others have used these techniques to deliver results.

We're going to cover public relations in the offline world even more – a complete video that delivers a step-by-step process for getting press coverage, writing effective press releases and finding the right magazines and journals, and ways to come up with the content. I'm going to explain the best way for you to approach an editor, and a bunch of case studies will underpin everything I talk through.

I'm going to show you the power of direct mail. It's overlooked by so many. But when you see some of the techniques we've been using to drive traffic to our online businesses, you'll be amazed at how effective it can be.

In fact, you might even find that buying a list of qualified prospects costs less and converts better then your current AdWords campaigns.

We're even going to cover how to set up an offline auto-responder series using postcards, greeting cards and three-folds to market your business – all on auto-pilot. It's the quickest way I know to marketing your business offline

All of these techniques sound time-consuming, don't they? And I suspect you've not got time to execute these ideas. So there's no point in learning them, right?

WRONG!

Another reason for developing this programme is because I wanted to share how the implementation of these concepts can become embedded in your day. Sceptics amongst you won't believe me! Well, you'll have to see for yourself how possible it is to embed these ideas into existing processes – and I'll show you how we do it in our businesses.

I'm going to show you how you can easily implement systems to use and leverage what you're already doing in your "online marketing" to reach these offline marketplaces.

How do we deliver this programme?

I've joined forces with the awesome training video production folks from The 8.45 Club to bring to you a new style of teaching.

You lead a busy life, yes?

You have a ton of reports, videos and DVDs sat on a shelf unwatched, yes?

Well this style of teaching is VERY different. Because you don't have time for fluff, do you?

We will deliver bite-sized chunks of seriously practical, engaging video, links and other resources for you to follow up with, into your inbox every 48 hours for the next eight weeks.

PLUS, get direct and personal access to me.

This isn't a "purchase and be left to your own devices" programme. Unlike a book, with GoingAnalogue.com, you'll find me interacting with members throughout the course –

answering their questions. I've even provided MP3 audio responses of ideas to participants along the way.

The more involved the community is, the more you'll get from me!

There's another business waiting to snatch your customers – and he's too smart to ignore the analog world.

So if you enjoyed this book and are planning of taking massive action to grow your business, boost your online traffic and increase conversion rates by using proven OFFLINE marketing techniques, then head over to GoingAnalogue.com right now and join us.

And as a thank-you for investing in Media Strategies for Internet Marketing and taking action, I want to refund the cost of this book. When you join us at www.GoingAnalogue.com, make sure you use the coupon code mediastrategies20, and you'll save 20% off the enrolment investment.

I really do look forward to hearing about your offline marketing success – be it from this book, GoingAnalogue.com or any other offline marketing techniques you implement, so please keep in touch.

Firstly, you could e-mail me via support@preneurgroup.com.

Hit me up on Twitter @preneur.

Join me on Facebook over www.facebook.com/preneurmarketing.

Or either on my two websites www.PreneurMarketing.com and www.PeteWilliams.com.au.

Speak soon,
Pete

BONUS 1:

Going Analogue's Press Release Distribution Video

Press release? Check. Bio sheet? Check. Q&A sheet? Check. You've now learned all you need to know about writing a press release so that you can get noticed. The key to success now is distribution.

Discover:

- How to send out the press release
- What sending options you have depending on your budget
- What his *recommended* and *tested* press release distribution services are

BONUS 2:

Unleashing the Power of Publicity's Dan Janal Interview

Dan Janal is an internationally recognized speaker, Internet marketer and best-selling author. As president of Janal Communications, he conducts strategic planning seminars and consultations for clients ranging for start-ups to Fortune 1000. Dan was on the PR team that launched America Online, the #1 online service, and personally directed the PR launch of Grolier's Electronic Encyclopedia, the first consumer software program ever produced on a CD-ROM.

Find out:

- How publicity made AOL the world's largest ISP
- How to get journalists calling you for interviews
- How to deal with reporters successfully
- How to construct powerful releases

BONUS 3:

Going Analogue's Buying Direct Mail Lists Session

No doubt you're very familiar with buying e-mail lists for your online marketing activities. Pete interviews an expert on how to do the same with physical addresses and why this can be so valuable.

Discover:

- How to buy a list
- What questions you should be asking when buying a list
- How you could sell your own list and rent it out to other people

Grab all these bonuses for FREE.
Go to www.MediaStrategiesForInternetMarketers.com NOW!

About the Author

Pete Williams is the author of *How to Turn Your Million-Dollar Idea Into a Reality* and *The Ultimate Press Release Swipe File: 50 Templates That You Can Use to Get Your Business Media Exposure Today*. Dubbed as "Australia's Richard Branson" in media publications all over the continent, he was just 21 when he sold Australia's version of the Yankee Stadium, The Melbourne Cricket Ground, for under $500.

He is the founder of several companies including Infiniti Telecommunications, On Hold Advertising, Simply Headsets and Preneur Group. He has been named the Global Runner-Up in the JCI Creative Young Entrepreneur Awards for 2009, the Southern Region Finalist in the Ernst & Young 2010 Entrepreneur of the Year and a member of Smart Companies: Top 30 Under 30.

Pete is also an international speaker, a marketing consultant and a faculty member of one the world's largest internet marketing training academies, the Thirty Day Challenge.